**TIME INC. HOME ENTERTAINMENT**
**Publisher** Richard Fraiman
**Executive Director, Marketing Services** Carol Pittard
**Director, Retail & Special Sales** Tom Mifsud
**Marketing Director, Branded Businesses** Swati Rao
**Director, New Product Development** Peter Harper
**Assistant Financial Director** Steven Sandonato
**Prepress Manager** Emily Rabin
**Product Manager** Victoria Alfonso
**Associate Book Production Manager** Suzanne Janso
**Associate Prepress Manager** Anne-Michelle Gallero

**Special thanks:** Bozena Bannett, Alexandra Bliss, Glenn Buonocore, Bernadette
Corbie, Robert Marasco, Brooke McGuire, Jonathan Polsky, Ilene Schreider, and
Adriana Tierno

Copyright 2005 ©Time Inc. Home Entertainment

Published by Time Inc. Home Entertainment

**TIME INC.**
1271 Avenue of the Americas
New York, New York 10020

ISBN: 1-932994-44-0
Time Inc. Home Entertainment is a trademark of Time Inc.

We welcome your comments and suggestions about Time Inc. Home Entertainment.
Please write to us at:
Time Inc. Home Entertainment
Attention: Book Editors
PO Box 11016
Des Moines, IA 50336-1016

**Grant Schneider would like to thank:**
Jo-Anne and Martin Schneider
Lawrence Diamond
Margot and Graydon Schneider Diamond
Ann Moore
Nora McAniff
Robin Domeniconi
TIWG Research and Marketing colleagues

**Design by** Georgia Rucker, for Downtown Bookworks Inc.

by Grant J. Schneider

# she
# means
# business

7

NEW RULES

**for marketing
to today's
woman**

# Contents

# Foreword

"If you know what women want, you can rule." Although this was said by a fictional character in the film *What Women Want*, it certainly rings true in business today. My job — running the Time Inc. Women's Group of magazines, which are read by over 45 million women every month — has made me particularly sensitive to this fact. Today, women are the most influential force in the American consumer economy. Moreover, women are not just supporting businesses from the checkout line, they are running them from the boardroom. *She Means Business* isn't just a play on words, it's an absolute reality in the marketplace today. But determining "what women want" is a complex proposition. I see fresh evidence all the time that there are not many things that all women agree upon. A "given" to a new mom in Manhattan might seem like utter nonsense to a grandmother in Grand Rapids.

In order to produce magazines that are consistently relevant and of value to our readers, it is important to understand the essential truths of their lives. And that requires research. Every year,

Time Inc. conducts over 1,000 research projects worldwide — surveys, focus groups, and large-scale studies. We intensely examine consumers, both those who read our magazines and those who don't. What we learn, along with the knowledge of our talented editors and marketers, gives us tremendous insight into the interests and concerns of consumers. After all, our magazines aren't just invited into readers' homes — we're invited into their lives. We reflect who they are. If we break that bond, our invitation is cancelled. So these insights are incredibly important to us.

The depth, breadth, and diversity of our women's research, in particular, gives us a very thorough understanding of women's attitudes and behaviors on such wide-ranging topics as health, style, success, motherhood, personal relationships, and so much more. Our insight helps us produce the best and most successful women's publications in the business. But you don't have to be a magazine publisher to appreciate the fascinating findings detailed in this book. *She Means Business* is our opportunity to share what we see as the forces and ideas that are shaping women's lives right now. Remember, this is not an effort to explain what "every woman" wants. (Anyone who offers you that probably has a bridge to sell you, too!) Rather, it's a detailed group portrait, with thousands of women each adding their own brushstrokes, resulting in a beautiful, unusual, and valuable representation of American women today.

Nora McAniff
Exective Vice President, Time Inc.

*Introduction:*

# The Rules
# Keep Changing

The following list of seven rules comes from a 1950s home economics textbook that was intended to prepare high school girls for the demands of married life. We keep it filed under "Y," as in, " Yo u ' ve come a long way, baby. "

**1** *Have dinner ready* Plan ahead, even the night before, to have a delicious meal — on time. This is a way of letting him know that you have been thinking about him and are concerned about his needs.

**2** *Prepare yourself* Take fifteen minutes to rest so you will be refreshed when he arrives. Touch up your makeup, put a ribbon in your hair, and be fresh looking.

**3** *Clear away clutter* Just before your husband arrives, gather up schoolbooks, toys, paper, etc. Then run a dust cloth over the tables. Your husband will feel he has reached a haven of rest and order, and it will give you a lift, too.

*4 Prepare the children.* Take a few minutes to wash the children's hands and faces, comb their hair, and, if necessary, change their clothes. They are little treasures, and he would like to see them playing the part.

*5 Make him comfortable.* Have him lean back in a comfortable chair or suggest he lie down in the bedroom. Have a cool drink ready for him. Arrange his pillow and offer to take off his shoes. Speak in a low, soft, soothing, and pleasant voice.

*6 Listen to him.* You may have a dozen things to tell him, but the moment of his arrival is not the time. Let him talk first.

*7 Make the evening his.* Never complain if he does not take you out to dinner or to other places of entertainment; instead, try to understand his world of strain and pressure and his need to be home and relax.

Was anyone's life ever really like this — an episode of *Leave It to Beaver* on steroids? Let's get real. The rules on this list are as quaintly obsolete for today's woman as typewriter ribbons and carbon paper are for someone using a laptop. As we stand here just across the threshold of the twenty-first century, nothing could be clearer than the fact that the truisms of fifty years ago no longer apply. (Apologies to all the "little treasures" and thirsty husbands with aching feet.) But that doesn't mean that there aren't any rules at all for women today. At the Time Inc. Women's Group of magazines, we devote enormous amounts of time and energy to locating the key issues and concerns that drive women's lives — we explore what is important to women, what frustrates them, what intrigues them, what fulfills them.

It's easy to talk about women using the old, familiar generalizations, but the truth of women's lives can only be found in the details. To succeed, one must understand that successful communication is a two-way street. We don't simply send information to our readers—we also get information back from them. Lots of it. This allows us to create publications that directly address issues of genuine concern to our audience, making our diverse constellation of magazines the most reader-friendly, up-to-date, and trusted brands in the business. Reaching over 45 million women a year, the Time Inc. Women's Group is the industry leader in giving women what they want through magazines including *People, Parenting, Cooking Light, Essence, InStyle, Teen People, Health, BabyTalk, Real Simple, People en Español, All You, Cottage Living,* and *Suede.* This book can show you how to do the same — whether you're trying to market to women or develop products or services targeting them, or simply want to communicate more effectively with them.

## American women at a glance

- **140 million** women make up 50.9% of total U.S. population.
- Average life expectancy: 79.7 years.
- **84 million** women work outside the home, making up 46.3% of the labor force.
- **56%** of all bachelor's degrees and 57% of all master's degrees are earned by women.
- **49%** of professional/managerial positions are held by women.
- **23%** of professional wives earn more than their husbands.
- **53%** of all voters are women.

(Sources: U.S. Census Bureau and *Health* magazine)

This book explores what women are interested in, focused on, and wanting today. While a woman's world in the 1950s was centered on the home, now her life is also about work and relationships and finding success in her own personal way. Today's values reflect the truth that "home" is just one part of the journey that women are taking every day, encountering a wealth of new opportunities, problems, and choices at every turn. In this book, we will be exploring the seven aspects of life that are the most important to women today: Balance, Time, Optimism, Trust, Expression, Control, and Connection. We'll examine the research that shows how and why each of these areas is vitally important to women's lives, we'll consider what these focal points mean for individual women and for society at large, and we'll suggest the implications of our findings for marketers, entrepreneurs, and others who are seeking to better understand and serve the needs of women.

### women at work

- 1960: 36% of women work outside the home.
- 2000: 58% of women work outside the home.

(Source: U.S. Census Bureau)

### how we know what we know

The ideas in these pages reflect the findings of dozens of proprietary research studies involving more than 30,000 American women conducted by the Time Inc. Women's Group. Thanks to comprehensive focus groups, telephone and online surveys, panels, and other large-scale surveys resulting in over 17,000 individual data points, this research offers an unparalleled opportunity to gain specific information about the most diverse, self-aware, and economically influential force in today's consumer marketplace, not to mention the world in general. Now we invite you to join us on our journey and to share in our findings, putting the power of our information and insights to work for you.

### hear me roar

Women are responsible for **85%** of Americans' annual $7 trillion in total personal expenditures. In 1996, no products specifically aimed at women were launched, compared with 32 in 2000 and 40 in 2001.

(Source: *Advertising Age*)

# *Balance*

Balance is something we desire in almost every aspect of our lives, from our checkbooks to our diets to the pH of our shampoos. It is also a buzzword that comes up whenever the issues confronting today's women are discussed. But what does "balance" really mean in the context of a busy life? Are we talking about the balance between work and home? Between husband and children? Between the attention paid to a toddler and to a newborn? Or between a woman's own needs

> "We can be sure that the greatest hope for maintaining equilibrium in the face of any situation rests within ourselves."
>
> —Francis J. Braceland

and those of all the people who depend on her? In truth, women's lives are less about balance than they are about multitasking — fulfilling many roles and completing many tasks all at the same time.

It comes as no surprise that women are struggling to find ways to manage their numerous responsibilities without leaving anyone (including themselves) feeling neglected and that many are often overwhelmed by the wide range of simultaneous demands being placed on them. What may be a surprise, however, is that most women wouldn't have it any other way. The vast majority of research reveals that women recognize and appreciate the fact that our society has evolved to allow women endless life options outside the home. As difficult as achieving "balance" can be, most women have no desire to go back to a time when balance wasn't an issue — because that would mean returning to a time when women were expected to devote 100% of their time to home and family. What they do desire is practical help in making the different pieces of their lives operate more efficiently and cooperatively.

### all in a day's work

- **90%** of women surveyed say they feel their career and personal life are well balanced right now.

- **81%** of working women say they would still want to work even if they didn't need to.

- **41%** say they work too many hours now.

(Source: *Real Simple*, "Values and Behavior Outlook")

## how motherhood changes everything

Issues of balance come dramatically front and center in a woman's life with the birth of a child. To explore this pivotal life stage, the Time Inc. Parenting Group invited mothers from all across the United States to join a nationally representative, interactive research community called The Mom Connection. Since 2003, the 8,000 Mom Connection members have responded to more than thirty surveys and polls, and their comments map the changes that occur throughout the parenting process. Nearly 60% of the members are either employed or on temporary leave, and of the 40% who quit work to stay home, 55% say they wish they could find a way to combine parenting with a job or career. This marks a dramatic 41% increase over the percentage with that wish only four years ago.

"How we spend our days is, of course, how we spend our lives."
—Annie Dillard

Obviously, the decisions women face regarding work and family are enormously complicated. Even though most women don't envy earlier generations whose lives revolved exclusively around their homes, they are only too aware that a happy balance is elusive and hard to sustain. Many questions arise. What will the impact be on her career if she decides to take a year or two off when a child is born? If she goes back to work right away, will she regret it later? Will her children feel neglected? What effect would the loss of her income have on her family's financialsecurity? Will she feel isolated and unfulfilled if she leaves the workforce? For all the talk of fifty-fifty parenting and men taking equal responsibility for kids and home, these are the types of issues that women confront to a far greater extent than men.

Studies suggest that there is still a long way to go before responsibility for household tasks is equally shared between partners. Research conducted by the General Merchandise Distributors Council (GMDC) Educational Foundation (an organization advising grocery store and drugstore owners), for instance, revealed that in spite of the dramatic increase in two-income households, 81% of the transactions in supermarkets still involve a woman. This has remained fairly constant over

the years. Furthermore, household decisions on diet, food products, over-the-counter health items, and general medical issues are typically made by the female head of the household: 86% of American women surveyed by *Cooking Light* describe themselves as the "primary decision maker/purchaser" in their household.

### men who hold their own

. . . . . . . . . . . . . . . . . . . . . . . . . . . . . . . . . . . . . . . . . . . . .

*Parenting* and *BabyTalk* magazines asked moms how much help they get from their spouses. The percentage who said their spouses shoulder at least half the burden in various task is as follows:

- Maintenance of home/auto/yard, etc. **80%**
- Leisure/play time with children **56%**
- Finances **40%**
- Family meal preparation **32%**
- Grocery shopping  **31%**
- Helping children with homework **29%**
- Household tasks (laundry/cleaning) **28%**
- Baby care **27%**
- Taking children to activities **23%**

(Source: Time Inc. Parenting Group, The Mom Connection)

. . . . . . . . . . . . . . . . . . . . . . . . . . . . . . . . . . . . . . . . . . . . .

Less often appreciated are the long-term, societal repercussions that result from the choices women are asked to make in their quest for balance. For example, consider their impact on the thorny (and often misunderstood) issue of the "wage gap" between men and women.

## the facts and fiction behind the wage gap

It has been widely reported that the wage gap between the sexes is narrowing. The numbers probably look familiar: in 1979, according to the Bureau of Labor Statistics, working women made 63% as much money as men. By 2002, it was reported that women's wages had risen dramatically, to 78% of men's. Even better, we were reassuringly told, the actual gap is even narrower, because that 78% figure doesn't take into account a larger gap among older women in the workforce that will soon disappear.

### show me the money

- Only 3% of the Fortune 500 top earners are women — even though women are 52% of the population and almost 50% or the workforce.

- Women make up only 13% of the top executive ranks of media, tele-communications and e-companies and only 9% of their boards. And of these women, only 3% had the titles of CEO, COO, president, or executive vice president.

(Source: *Advertising Age*)

Sounds encouraging, right? Unfortunately, according to groundbreaking new research by economists Stephen J. Rose and Heidi Hartmann, as reported in the *New York Times*, the 78% figure is a substantial overstatement. One big reason is that, in reality, women are more likely to work fewer hours than men and often feel compelled to drop out of the workforce for years at a time, usually for child rearing and to tend to family. The reported wage gap only takes into account the earnings of those women who work full-time for a full year — about half of working women in any single year. When Rose and Hartmann compared the actual earnings of men and women from 1983 to 1998 in the prime working years between ages 26 and 59, they found that the pay gap was not narrowing at all. Over that period, women on average earned only 38% of what men did; the average woman earned $273,592 over 15 years, compared with $722,693 for the average man.

> "One cannot collect all the beautiful shells on the beach. One can collect only a few, and they are more beautiful if they are few."

—Anne Morrow Lindbergh

Okay, one might say, if women tend to work fewer hours or take time off to raise children, they will earn less money. But the economists' analysis turned up evidence of far larger, more systemic inequalities. A much higher proportion of women have had jobs that pay at the bottom of the income scale, and fewer of them ever climb to higher-quality jobs. Women of all educational backgrounds also predominantly take different kinds of jobs than men — jobs that pay less. All this creates a vicious cycle of sorts. Because wives usually earn less than their husbands, they are far more likely to give up their jobs to care for children. Then, when they do return to work after having children, they very often take low-paying temporary or part-time jobs that provide few (if any) benefits so they can be home for their families as needed. This in turn consistently guarantees a large pool of low-paid labor, encouraging companies to use such workers rather than to create better jobs. Furthermore, the

## swinging singles are no cause for alarm

Dire warnings that the traditional family unit is dying out were sparked by recent findings that less than one-fourth of American households consist of married parents and their kids. Yes, that figure reflects an important societal trend, but it's not that families are on the way out. While the percentage of kids living with a single parent has risen in the last two decades, about seven in ten still live with a pair of married parents. What has really changed is the rise in households consisting of one person — often a young person who hasn't yet married but probably will. Census data in 1978 put the median age of first marriages at 24.2 for men and 21.8 for women. By 2002, the age had climbed to 26.9 for men and 25.3 for women. This means a lot more single twentysomethings living large in one-person households.

(Source: *Adweek*)

unspoken assumption that women will drop out of the work-force leads American businesses to underinvest in women's careers and to tend to hire them for dead-end jobs.

Will the gender disparity in wages ever vanish? The good news is a countervailing force has emerged: a gender gap in education that actually favors women. Among Americans aged 25–34, census figures show that women are now more likely than men to have finished college (33% versus 29%). If current trends continue, it is estimated that there will be 156 women per 100 men earning degrees by 2020. The change among minority women is even more striking: a recent report from the American Council on Education shows that among college-age African-American women who've graduated from high school, the college participation rate rose from 28.4% in 1978–1980 to 42% in 1998–2000. Among Hispanic women, the rate rose from 27% to 37%.

*what she wants*
*recognize the value*
*of housekeeping*

Consumers everywhere are grateful that technology is making daily household chores less of a burden. But marketers of new, timesaving home products should keep in mind that even the most mundane tasks often carry important meanings. The rituals of homemaking quietly serve as outward manifestations of the nurturing, fortifying relationships that are at the core of family life. When marketing products that make house-work less laborious, be careful not to imply that the work itself is unimportant. (Spouses, children, and anyone else who gets to enjoy the benefits of living in a well kept home should bear this lesson in mind as well.) In caring for our homes, we are caring for each other.

Other statistics bear out the fact that women are much more likely than men to feel the need to tailor their work life to meet the demands of family, even if that means taking a lower-paying or part-time job. In a recent Kaiser Family Foundation survey, 49% of working mothers said they have to miss work when a child is home sick, versus only 30% of working fathers. About 80% of mothers said they "assume the major role in selecting their children's doctor, taking children to doctor's appointments, and follow-up care." One of the reasons many women have trouble finding time for themselves is that they have a tendency to make time for themselves only after everyone else's needs have been satisfied. They find it difficult to say no to other people.

"Basically women work alone when they're at home. They think no one is feeling what they are feeling, that no one understands their daily frustrations. But we do; we all do."

—Erma Bombeck

## homemakers are home — working

It is important to realize that women who do not have jobs outside the home are constantly facing the need to balance conflicting agendas and demands, too. Indeed, for most women and for increasing numbers of men, home is in many senses of the word a workplace, not some sort of storybook haven from the pressures of the outside world. There is real work involved in housekeeping, getting food on the table, keeping rooms and clothes and children clean, driving carpools and helping with school projects, and looking out for everyone's health and well-being. Professor and author Mary Catherine Bateson points out that even though we are always looking for ways to streamline or eliminate the mechanics of these jobs, the daily tasks of "homemaking" have a value that goes beyond their immediate results. She says, "We enact and strengthen our relationships by performing dozens of small practical rituals, setting the table, making coffee, raking the lawn — giving and receiving material tokens, even in a household of servants . . . . Marriage creates work, far beyond the apparent practical need, in order that work may create marriage."

"Women need solitude in order to find again the true essence of themselves."

**—Anne Morrow Lindbergh**

While it may be difficult to appreciate this when facing the day's eighth load of laundry or third round of meal preparations, Bateson makes an intriguing case that old-fashioned distinctions between work and home (usually along gender lines) are likely to shift as new kinds of family life become common. With increasing numbers of people working from home as entrepreneurs or freelancers, with the demands of the workplace no longer confined to the hours between 9 a.m. and 5 p.m., it is probable that men will come to share women's sense of the importance of balancing the personal and professional parts of daily life, and maybe even come to see it as a blessing. Reflecting on her own experience juggling being a mother, a college professor, and the former dean of the faculty at Amherst College, Bateson says, "Increasingly, during the years of being a working mother and searching for quality time with my daughter, I have become convinced that the best times actually occur in the kitchen or the car, when some simple task like shelling peas or getting to the supermarket defines the time and space in which to build and strengthen our communication."

### what she wants
a mini facial

Women are looking for ways to nurture and pamper themselves that do not necessarily require an enormous investment of time or money. Find ways to help them see that by making the effort to take care of themselves, they will be better equipped to take care of the people around them they love. This does not mean that a woman must go to a spa for two weeks to unwind; she would also be happy indulging in a luxury beauty product, enjoying a massage or a facial, or taking a night off to go to a movie with an old friend.

A woman's role is to function as the family command center. She arbitrates and negotiates all conflicts between family members — and likely between friends and business associates, too. Consumer trend forecaster and business consultant Faith Popcorn likens a woman's job to that of United Nations ambassador. Since she takes both her emotional and her practical responsibilities seriously, at times she will find herself faced with seemingly impossible choices, like being expected to leave the bedside of a sick loved one because she has just landed a big account, or staying late to finish an urgent business proposal, even though she has a dozen guests coming for dinner.

> "There is a time for work. And a time for love. That leaves no other time."
> —Coco Chanel

It is important to recognize the very real dangers that come attached to feeling that one's life is out of balance. Why, for example, is depression a problem for five times as many women as men? Therapist Mira Kirschenbaum suggests it is because " women are five times less likely to say ' yes' to themselves than men are. The self gets worn out by our not doing a good job of taking care of it. If you don't take care of yourself, you'll stop thinking of yourself as someone who has a lot to give. Instead, you'll feel deprived. How can you give others joy if you can't give yourself joy ? "

While all parents are sometimes prone to feeling a lack of balance in their lives, it is women who are most susceptible to the problem, whether they are working outside the home or not. Women in every generation have talked about this quality of dividedness in their lives, long before they were balancing ten-hour days at a law practice and the running of a home. Bateson makes the point that in our society women are expected to give in to multiple, conflicting demands on their time, but men are not. In *Composing a Life*, she writes of what comes from these differing expectations: "Women have been regarded as unreliable because they are torn by multiple commitments; men become capable of true dedication when they are either celibate, in the old religious model, with no family to distract them, or have families organized to provide support but not distraction, the little woman behind the great man."

Perhaps, though, Bateson goes on to suggest, we're looking at this all wrong. What if rather than being "unreliable" because they must choose between multiple commitments, women are actually "representing a higher wisdom? Perhaps we can discern in women honoring multiple commitments a new level of productivity and new possibilities of learning."

### what she wants
bliss, not bucks

Since so many women are inner-focused, it's important to communicate in a language and on a level that they relate to. When marketing to women, rather than using the traditional vocabulary of success that focuses on external symbols of power and status, try incorporating the themes of emotional success that women now embrace: peace of mind, happiness, fulfillment, balance, faith. This insight should also inform the types of products and services you try to sell to women.

## feeling good is the new beemer

Bateson's notion that while striving for life balance, women live, learn, and uncover new possibilities is borne out by the results of a landmark study conducted by *Real Simple* magazine. To explore women's feelings about success, respondents were asked to identify specific elements that are important to their own vision of a successful life; six key areas emerged:

- happy children (81%)
- close relationships (77%)
- a comfortable and inviting home (68%)
- an enjoyable career (62%)
- a healthy spiritual life (62%)
- intellectual growth (62%)

These responses are striking not only for the wide range of life areas they cover but also for their strong emotional component. For example, while 81% cited "having happy children" as very important, only 57% cited "having successful children." Even more revealing, the vast majority said that "having a home that is comfortable and inviting" is very important (68%), but

### I need to relax!

When they want to pamper themselves, women surveyed by *InStyle* reported that they get a pedicure (68%) or a manicure (60%). Nearly half also get massages (49%) or buy new lipstick (48%).

(Source: InStyle magazine, "Inside Style")

only one in ten said "owning a large, impressive home" is important. "Having a career you really enjoy" was widely seen as very important (62%), but "moving up in your career to a high level" was not frequently mentioned (25%). When they spoke about success, the women in this study consistently and resoundingly emphasized the interior over the exterior, the emotional over the material. This emotional emphasis is even more evident in the words these women chose to describe their view of success. The six most frequently chosen words were happiness (80%), peace of mind (75%), fulfillment (71%), self-confidence (71%), freedom (70%), and balance (64%). Again, these women gravitated toward terms that reflect their emotional lives rather than toward more traditional, material, outward manifestations of success.

"I wish I could tell you that I had some scientific basis for being a woman executive or managing men versus women, but I don't. You just sort of intuitively do it, and try to do the best job that you can do and learn from your past experiences."

**—Meg Whitman**

# all women juggle

This acceptance of life's complexity as integral to achieving true success may be seen simultaneously as a hurdle for women and as a sign of Bateson's "higher wisdom."

## what's in a name?

The firm Reach Advisors asked mothers if the term "soccer mom" fit them, and if not, did they have a catchier phrase to describe their lives. Among their suggestions:

- I'm not your supermom
- Minivan maven
- Book-reading mom
- Taxi driver
- Domestic personality
- Child-rearing technician
- Stay-at-home-and-really-work mom

(Source: *The New York Times Magazine*)

When asked to identify the best strategy for a fulfilling life, more than half of the women in the *Real Simple* study chose " H aving children and also having a career" (52%), while only a third chose "Having children and staying home to raise them" (33%). Only 8% chose "Not having children and focusing on a career." (It is worth noting that the responses to this question were virtually identical for women with children under 18 and women in general.) They are not looking to make their lives less complicated by limiting the number of options open to them. These women associate being successful with the ability to balance the demands of home and career, not with making a choice between the two.

"To fulfill a dream, to be allowed to sweat over lonely labor, to be given a chance to create, is the meat and potatoes of life. The money is the gravy."

**—Bette Davis**

Other tangible benefits also come with embracing the reality that women can simultaneously fulfill multiple roles. Many wives and mothers who have gone back to school or started working outside the home find that rather than feeling exhausted, they experience a new sense of vitality. Anyone who enjoys regular physical exercise will understand this phenomenon. In theory, a tough workout seems like it would lead to fatigue or exhaustion, but instead it usually leads to a feeling of having more energy and strength. So it can be with the rest of life. Susan Nolen-Hoeksema, a professor of psychology at the University of Michigan, writes that when a woman broadens her base of self-esteem and social support by having multiple activities and interests, it is critical to her well-being, and it can be beneficial to her children's well-being as well. She explains,

# "Always aim for achievement, and forget about success."

**—Helen Hayes**

"When a mother is focused singularly on her children, they can feel smothered . . . . Having multiple roles gives a woman a base to fall back on in times of trouble in her family."

The benefits of a balanced life can flow in the other direction, too, improving an individual's performance in the workplace. When Boston psychologist Rosalind Barnett studied 300 dual-earner couples, she found that men and women who were in satisfying relationships were better able than unattached people to withstand workplace stress. It seems that strong personal relationships provide a form of support that carries over beyond the home. Another study, this one conducted by the Center for Human Resources at the Wharton School, found that those males and females graduating from high school in 1972 who said that they valued having a strong family life earned more money over the next fourteen years than their classmates who didn't. Both of these studies must make us question the longstanding notion that work and relationships necessarily pull in opposite directions.

In her book *Toxic Work*, Barbara Reinhold draws on her experience as the director of the career development office and a professor of psychology at Smith College. Reinhold conducted research with Smith College alumnae, surveying nearly 1,700 women in a range of fields and at different levels in organizations. Eighty-nine percent of the mothers surveyed reported that their experiences as parents had made them more effective in the workplace. In particular, they felt they had developed "critical managerial strategies such as coaching, staying calm in crisis situations, and rewarding incremental improvements in performance. "

Employed people belong to more civic groups than those who are outside the paid workforce. And, surprisingly, working longer hours is linked to more, not less, civic involvement. That's likely because those who work long hours spend an average of 30% less time watching television, which even after a long workday still leaves them more time for social interaction and community involvement.

The multifaceted lives of women suggest a new way of handling the reality of the complicated, often ambiguous world in which we all live today. In seeking balance, rejecting the notion that they must make "either/or" choices in their lives, women are also rejecting the idea that life is a zero-sum game,

where spending time on a career necessarily means being less involved at home. Instead of finding that one choice replaces another, one choice can enhance another. Resources and energy can increase as they are used, and success in one part of life can fuel success in the others. Yes, today's women understand that they can't "have it all." However, their successes offer proof that they can create lives that are full and fulfilling.

●  ●  ●  ●  ●  ●

*what she wants*
to be celebrated and appreciated for her many roles
As a general rule, women are not nostalgic for the world of previous generations — a world they perceive as offering few routes to success for women. They relish the variety of options available to them, but recognize that having more options necessarily puts new demands on their time and energy. To reach a woman, communicate that you understand both the hurdles and the rewards facing women today. Celebrate the rich diversity of their current lives and you'll be on your way to connecting more powerfully.

●  ●  ●  ●  ●  ●

# *Time*

Closely related to the issue of balance is that of time. For many women today, there rarely seems to be enough of it to go around. In fact, time is the single most important resource that people have nowadays, according to DYG Inc., one of the nation's leading research organizations. Because everything in life takes time, it becomes part of the balancing act of what we take on and what we skip, constantly quantifying the worth of a visit, a meal, or a trip to a store. Today, most women find time in high demand so the issue affects how women handle their finances, shopping habits, eating patterns, exercise routines (or lack thereof!), social outings, sleep, and overall health. We have all been in a situation where you would love to meet a friend for lunch, but felt that the time it would take to shower, change and ready yourself, find the car keys, drive across town, order, chat, eat, wait for and pay the bill, and drive back home was just too great. One seemingly simple lunch might pre-clude you from crossing several things off the to-do list in your head, so instead, you opted for a quick bite at the deli or fast food in the car between errands.

A small finding taken from a study conducted by *Real Simple* magazine speaks to the extraordinary value of time in a big way: women spend an average of 55 minutes a day just looking for things. Think about it. That is an hour of the waking day lost. (Maybe that missing hour is the thing we should be looking for!) Is it a surprise that when DYG asked women to choose between gain-ing additional moderate amounts of time or of money, they picked more time by nearly two to one?

*Real Simple* conducts frequent "Problem Detector" research, surveying women across the country to find out what specific issues and general life areas are causing them trouble. The responses help the editors of *Real Simple* make certain that the magazine is cover-ing topics that are of particular interest to its readers. This research has led to special issues like *Real Simple*'s annual organization cover story, since being better organized is a prime area about which women want practical strategies and suggestions. Almost every problem that emerges in the survey can be linked, directly or indi-rectly, to time.

## real problems facing real women

. . . . . . . . . . . . . . . . . . . . . . . . . . . . . . . . . . . . . . . . . . . . . . . . . . . .

When women rank their specific concerns in the *Real Simple* Problem Detector, some general themes emerge, such as,

Money

- I'm spending too much money, not saving enough. (#1)
- I'm not prepared for unexpected financial events. (#3)

Exercise

- I can't stay motivated to exercise, and once I get out of an exercise routine it's hard to get back into it. (#5)
- As I get older it takes longer to see the results from exercise (#10).
- I don't have enough energy to exercise. (#11)

Food

- I feel too tired to cook when I get home from work. (#6)
- I find that I don't cook healthy foods as much as I should because it takes too long. (#14)

Overload

- It's hard to be in the moment because there's always something else on my mind. (#18)

(Source: *Real Simple*, "Problem Detector")

. . . . . . . . . . . . . . . . . . . . . . . . . . . . . . . . . . . . . . . . . . . . . . . . . . . .

With all the innovations and improvements in technology, why are we so busy today? Weren't these devices supposed to make work easier and give us more leisure time? Well, that may have been the idea, but it hasn't quite worked out that way. Consider what happened following the arrival of computers in the workplace. Thanks to computers, workers are vastly more productive now than they were twenty years ago, but they are still working just as hard over as many hours, if not even harder over more hours. Technology has increased expectations of productivity rather than decreased hours of labor. No doubt our great-grandmothers were similarly surprised to discover that the arrival of the mechanical washing machine did not allow them to spend less total time washing clothes; it just made it possible (and expected) to change linens and clothes many times more often. Somehow the work expands to fill the time; we are constantly busy, to the point of doing as many things at the same time as possible. We talk on our cell phones while driving to the store, we check our e-mail while jogging on the treadmill, we skim the newspaper while helping a child with homework and cooking dinner. To use our time most productively, we fill every available minute with as many activities as possible.

"I have a simple philosophy. Fill what's empty. Empty what's full. Scratch where it itches."

—Alice Roosevelt Longworth

## time flies when you're having kids

In its "What Really Matters to Moms" research, *Parenting* magazine asked mothers to rank 208 different statements according to how intensely and how frequently each bothered them and how much they wanted help in addressing it. Many interesting trends emerge, including,

### EBBING ENERGY

- I don't feel refreshed when I wake up in the morning. (#3)
- I feel tired all the time. (#6)

### ATTENTION BREAKS

- I have trouble completing tasks or projects that I start. (#47)
- My child interrupts when I try to get things done. (#49)

### FEELING OVERWHELMED

- I find it difficult to concentrate because there's so much to do. (#50)
- I can't relax because there's so much that needs to get done. (#7)

### GUILT, PRESSURE, AND EXPECTATIONS

- I feel pressure to be as good a mother as my mother was. (#186)
- I have a hard time saying no when asked to help out with child-related or school activities. (#195)
- I feel guilty because going to work feels like a welcome break from being with my child. (#198)

## the foodie blues

In a 2003 survey, *Cooking Light* found that the mast majority of women consider "food preparation time" (75%) and "ease of preparation" (78%) to be key factors when they purchase groceries, which helps explain the rise in popularity of one-dish meals. Similarly, *InStyle* research revealed that 43% of women are extremely or very likely to pay more for prepared foods because they save time. The number one food-related problem to emerge from *Real Simple*'s surveys is that women are too tired to cook when they get home from work. This was far ahead of other, more widely talked about food challenges like reducing dietary fat and cutting back on carbs. Perhaps the true root cause of America's problem with obesity isn't what we are eating but why we are eating it. We're too pooped to cook healthy food!

### diet du jour

The majority of American women (54%) feel they receive too much conflicting information about which foods are healthy and which are not to make knowledgeable decisions.

(Source: *Cooking Light*, "*Cooking Light* Insight")

## you are what you eat

. . . . . . . . . . . . . . . . . . . . . . . . . . . . . . .

What motivates a healthy diet?

- More time to cook (55%)
- Already eat a healthy diet (47%)
- Healthy and tasty menus (45%)
- Having access to healthy recipes (29%)

(Source: *Health* magazine, "Women in Motion 2003")

. . . . . . . . . . . . . . . . . . . . . . . . . . . . . . .

More than ever before, issues of speed and convenience determine what we eat. Moms tell *Parenting* and *BabyTalk* that they face a tug-of-war between healthy, nutritious food choices and convenience. One telltale sign, as reported in *Adweek:* the proportion of at-home dinners in which the main dish is a frozen item (eaten after it's thawed, one assumes) reached 10.4% in 2000 — one-fifth higher than it was five years earlier. An NPDFoodworld report similarly documents a steady rise in Americans' consumption of frozen fare:

annual consumption
of frozen meals

1992: 55.7
1995: 63.1
1998: 69.5
2001: 74.0

In another indication of how today's consumers are streamlining meal preparation, the percentage of at-home dinners that included a side dish fell from 66% in 1991 to 56% in 2002. However, even though Americans are spending less time cooking, this has not resulted in an increase in dining out. The number of meals eaten in restaurants has remained almost constant over the years.

*what she wants*
fast healthy food

The vast majority of American women are seeking information and products that can help them to produce healthy, home-cooked meals with quick preparation time. Shortcuts and timesavers that don't affect a meal's overall healthiness or quality are the Holy Grail of today's kitchen.

## workouts are tough to work in . . . to my schedule

Much in the way time constraints have had a real impact on the way Americans shop for and prepare food, they have also affected exercise habits. *Cooking Light* found that 36% of women surveyed agree with the statement "It's a struggle to get myself to exercise regularly." Interestingly, when women do exercise, they often have an ulterior motive. The same survey found that women are 25% more likely than men to state that a major reason they exercise is "It gives me time for myself."

### I would exercise more if . . .

- Thought I would see results more quickly (69%).
- Had more free time (67%).
- Had a partner or group to exercise with (61%).
- Had work-out equipment at home (53%).
- Had a personal trainer (47%).
- Had more information about how to exercise properly (32%).

(Source: *Health* magazine, "Women in Motion 2003")

**only teens want to shop till they drop**

As pressed as we are for time, Americans manage to spend more time shopping than anyone else in the world. Americans go to shopping centers about once a week, and our nation has more shopping centers than high schools. Barry Schwartz, a professor of social theory at Swarthmore College, reports that in a recent survey, 93% of teenage girls said that shopping was their favorite activity. They should enjoy it while they can — the majority of working women say that shopping is a hassle, as do most men. When working women are asked to rank the pleasure they get from various activities, grocery shopping ranks next to last and other shopping is fifth from the bottom.

> ## "An unhurried sense of time is in itself a form of wealth."
>
> **—Bonnie Friedman**

Given the number of highly specialized products and the range of choices consumers are presented with, why hasn't shopping become easier — or at least more pleasurable — for us? In his book *The Paradox of Choice*, Schwartz points us toward an answer when he describes a fascinating study of consumer behavior that took place in a gourmet food store in an upscale community. The store frequently set up sample tables to promote new items, and for a few weeks they allowed researchers

*what she wants*
instant gratification

Readers surveyed by *InStyle* said they are unlikely to put themselves on a waiting list for a popular fashion or beauty item (19% fashion, 21% beauty). But roughly half will buy an item they really want on the spot, even though it's a splurge (50% fashion, 54% beauty). One of the secrets of *InStyle*'s own success is their insistence that the items featured in the magazine are available in stores and on Web sites, through resources that are printed right on the page.

(Source: *InStyle* magazine, "Inside Style")

to display a line of twenty-four high-quality jams. Customers who passed by could taste samples, and they were given a coupon for a dollar off if they bought a jar. In one variation of the study, six flavors of the jam were offered for tasting. In another, all twenty-four flavors were offered for tasting. In either case, the entire set of twenty-four was available for purchase. The large array of sample jams attracted more passers-by to the table than the small array, although in both cases people tended to taste about the same number of jams. When it came to buying, however, a huge difference became obvious. Thirty percent of the people exposed to the smaller array of jams actually bought a jar; only 3% of those exposed to the larger array of jams did so.

Why should this be the case? Schwartz suggests that a large array of options may actually discourage consumers "because it forces an increase in the effort that goes into making a decision. So consumers decide not to decide. Also, a large array of options may diminish the attractiveness of what people actually choose, the reason being that thinking about the attractions of some of the unchosen options detracts from the pleasure derived from the chosen one." In other words, the fact that our stores are so fabulously well stocked with countless varieties of every conceivable item may actually inhibit us from making purchases.

● ● ● ● ● ●

***what she wants***

the right to choose . . .

but not too many choices

Brand extension is one of the most potentially rewarding — and notoriously tricky — areas of business. Success is not determined solely by the intrinsic quality or appeal of the new product line. If faced with too many seemingly similar choices, consumers may respond by not making any choice at all. Manufacturers and marketers must be wary of splintering off too many variations of a successful brand. No matter how good the products are, forcing consumers to choose among too many varieties of a product is a recipe for lost sales.

● ● ● ● ● ●

In studying the behaviors and attitudes of young children, psychologist Susan Sugarman has found evidence that suggests humans as a species are not biologically equipped for the large number of choices we currently face. She points out that newborns and infants do not have to choose among options; they simply accept or reject whatever they are offered. The same is true of toddlers. "Do you want some juice? Would you like to go to the park?" Parents pose questions and toddlers answer with either a yes or a no. Then, when children have developed sufficient language skills, their parents begin asking them more complex questions, like "Do you want apple juice or milk?" "Do you want to go

## what she wants
freebies!

Since an overabundance of choices makes most consumers glaze over, it is now more difficult than ever to get shoppers to try a new brand or product, particularly in an already crowded area of the marketplace. When appropriate, free samples and trial offers are the most effective way of overcoming consumers' reluctance to choose. When the Time Inc. Parenting Group asked mothers what would influence them to try something different once they have found a product that works for them, moms ranked samples and coupons right below the advice of doctors and other moms. Over 95% reported using samples and coupons, whether buying products for themselves or for their children.

to the playground or the swimming pool?" Suddenly, "yes" or "no" will no longer suffice. Sugarman recounts one mother's description of the dilemma facing her five-year-old:

> I have noticed that my son sometimes has difficulty making the sorts of choices that exclude one thing or another. I have the sense that it has to do with a sense of loss. That choosing one thing over another will mean that one thing is lost. Finally making the choice somehow minimizes the pleasure in the thing that is gained, though there also seems to be an accompanying relief in finally making the choice. I have noticed him deliberating, as if he is frozen with indecision. Most recently, I noticed him doing this when given a choice between different colored popsicles.

## "I must govern the clock, not be governed by it."

—Golda Meir

Sugarman concludes, "Learning to choose is hard. Learning to choose well is harder. And learning to choose well in a world of unlimited possibilities is harder still, perhaps too hard."

● ● ● ● ● ●

### *what she wants*
#### time and energy

*Real Simple* found that women con-sider "lack of time" (74%) and "lack of energy" (63%) as far and away their greatest obstacles to achieving success. Marketers have a tremen-dous opportunity in offering women ways to help them feel more in control of these issues. Most women are on the lookout for any new products or services that will genuinely help them to meet these challenges.

(Source: *Real Simple* magazine, "A New Definition of Success")

● ● ● ● ● ●

As time becomes more precious, it stands to reason that we become increasingly frustrated by having to make so many choices all the time. Sugarman's story about the five-year-old child who finds it difficult to choose a popsicle flavor will likely res-onate with most adults who have stood in front of a wall of prod-ucts, each of which promises to make life easier, more satisfying, or more delicious in its own subtly different way. We are confronted with so many choices that it is impossible to research them adequately or to feel confident in our decisions. Time is rushing by, and we find ourselves either stalled in a state of confusion or making a random choice and hoping for the best. When the smallest details of our daily lives require choosing, it becomes more and more difficult to prioritize truly important issues that would benefit from serious time, attention, and rigorous consideration.

## when push comes to shove, we skimp on sleep

A dangerous side effect of our constant busyness and lack of time is that Americans today are sleeping less than those of past generations. A 2001 study conducted by the National Sleep Foundation found that fewer than one-third of Americans get the recommended eight hours of sleep a night. More than 30% say they sleep less than seven hours a night — with disturbing results. More than 40% of people surveyed said that they constantly feel tired and that not getting enough sleep interferes with their daily activities. Lack of sleep contributes to raising stress levels. And, according to the Harvard Mind-Body Institute, between 60% and 90% of doctor visits today are the result of stress-related complaints.

"All my possessions for a moment of time."
—Queen Elizabeth I

Lack of time is more than just a pesky annoyance—it affects the total quality of our lives. The continuous pressure of finding enough time to get everything done has a very real impact on women's overall health and well-being. It influences crucial decisions about food and exercise and impacts self-esteem. Helping women to be better organized and to make smart choices about how they prioritize the tasks they face is no minor task; doing so helps them to be healthier and more successful in everything they do.

# *Optimism*

Even in our most uncertain times — in the weeks and months after September 11, 2001, when the threat of terrorism cast a shadow over so many parts of our lives — Americans exhibit seemingly bottomless wellsprings of optimism. In periods of economic recession as well as the boom times, this deep and resilient strain of optimism can be seen as a particularly American character trait that affects our habits, traditions, and outlook on the world. According to a Roper survey, half of all Americans feel generally optimistic about the future of the country, while only 17% are pessimistic. (In contrast, twenty-five years ago, only 39% of Americans were optimistic about the future of the country.) The majority of Americans not only feel that life is good, but also that it will improve, according to a January 2004 Gallup poll. On a more personal level, *Real Simple* found that women generally express high levels of confidence in the direction their lives are moving and in their ability to make choices that best meet their needs. *Health* magazine's research shows that women are notably optimistic when it comes to their physical well-being: 85% said they were confident there will be cures for most life-threatening diseases in their lifetime. This optimistic outlook among women even affects *People* magazine's decisions about which stories to put on the cover every week. Hands down, the biggest newsstand sales are for covers featuring celebrity weddings and births. Contrary to popular belief, happy events attract more readers than tragic ones.

An optimistic outlook is a trait common to women of all ethnic backgrounds and age groups, but a study conducted by *Essence* magazine found that African-American women are particularly likely to describe themselves as self-confident and physically attractive — in fact, they are two to three times more likely than other women to give themselves high marks on a wide range of questions related to this subject.

### rose-colored glasses

In terms of how you look at life, do you usually see your glass as half empty or half full?

- 90% half full
- 10% half empty

(Source: *Real Simple,* "Values and Behavior Outlook")

## the essence of optimism

As compared with Caucasian women, African-American women are:

- Twice as likely to describe themselves as self-confident (66% vs. 34%).
- Twice as likely to say it's important always to look their best (65% vs. 32%).
- Three times as likely to describe themselves as sexy (34% vs. 9%).

(Source: *Essence* magazine, "Window on Our Women Report")

Psychologist Martin Seligman's research suggests an important correlation between an optimistic outlook and the likelihood of achieving success. He has found that optimists tend to explain their successes with chronic, global, and personal causes and failures with transient, specific, and universal ones. Pessimists do the exact opposite. For example, optimists say things like "I got an A" and "She gave me a C." Pessimists say things like "I got a C" and "He gave me an A." By finding chronic causes for failure, pessimists subconsciously expect failures to persist. By finding personal causes for success, optimists build greater self-esteem and are less likely to suffer from depression when confronted with a failure. Barbara Reinhold of Smith College has seen what this can mean in the workplace. "Expectation edits reality," she explains. "When your job doesn't fit and you view the problem as permanent, pervasive, and personalized, it's almost impossible to find the energy to do the work of arranging a change." In other words, optimism doesn't just make a bad situation seem bearable; it can be the key to getting ourselves out of that bad situation altogether. Optimism breeds success.

# "Children are likely to live up to what you believe of them."

**—Lady Bird Johnson**

More and more researchers are coming around to Seligman's idea that psychological traits, like optimism, are directly connected to tangible success. In her book *Necessary Dreams: Ambition in Women's Changing Lives,* psychiatrist Anna Fels writes, "Mood isn't usually mentioned in discussions of ambition, yet the qualities required for pursuing an ambition are intimately linked to mood. At the least, normal levels of energy, concentration, optimism, social confidence, as well as

*what she wants*
to be viewed through rose-colored glasses

Avoid portraying women as helpless victims of forces beyond their control; focus on the fulfilling aspects of their complex, multifaceted lives and not the stressful side. After all, today's women see many of the things that can make their lives so complicated as the very things that can bring them success and happiness.

assertiveness and a sense of capability are all required to pursue an ambition." She explains that pessimism and harsh self-criticism are typical characteristics of depression, and they make the achievement of one's ambitions virtually impossible.

"We must not . . . ignore the small daily differences we can make which, over time, add up to big differences that we often cannot foresee."

—Marian Wright Edelman

## it just keeps getting better

A woman's outlook on life can change over time. Among the entire group of women surveyed in *Real Simple*'s success study, there was an almost even split between those who agreed with the statement "With enough effort and drive a woman can be successful in all areas of life" (50%) and the statement "It is impossible for a woman to be successful in all areas . . . she needs to make trade-offs and focus" (48%). But when these responses are sorted by age group, we find that 62% of younger women (aged 25–34) believe that a woman can be successful in all areas of her life, versus only 43% of older women (over age 50). Similarly, 55% of older women say that trade-offs are necessary

for success, versus only 37% of younger women. It is likely that the older women would not necessarily consider themselves "less optimistic" in their views, but simply more realistic.

## like fine wine . . .

Even though we are used to hearing that we live in a youth-obsessed culture, women of all ages seem to feel that "the best is yet to come." When they were asked to identify the peak age for success in a woman's life, women aged 25–34 said 41 years old. Women aged 35–49 said 50 years old, and women over 50 said 58 years old. At any age, women believe there are opportunities for greater achievement in their future. *InStyle* magazine has learned that a younger face on its covers does not always equal bigger newsstand sales. In 2003, two of the bestselling *InStyle* covers featured longtime stars Meg Ryan (who was 42 at the time) and Julia Roberts (who was 37). By voting with their pocketbooks, readers proved that the celebrities that interest them most are not the youngest.

### the next generation of women will . . .

- Have more opportunities to get ahead in the workplace (95%).

- Be more financially independent and resourceful (94%).

- Be better able to take care of their own health (94%).

- Feel better about themselves and have higher self-esteem (88%).

- Have access to higher-quality healthcare (85%).

(Source: *Health* magazine, "Women in Motion 2001")

## ❸ ● ●

# "The way I see it, if you want the rainbow, you gotta put up with the rain."

**– Dolly Parton**

Women's optimism about future generations is surely a reflection of the enormous strides they have made in recent decades. They can look around today and see other women being successful in a myriad of situations, both personal and professional. Every successful woman becomes a model for others, giving rise to aspirations and dreams through the living example of her own accomplishments. Women can also draw inspiration from witnessing others overcoming all manner of obstacles and hurdles that appear before them.

● ● ● ● ● ●

***what she wants***
*individual attention*

**Women are independent thinkers with their own ideas about what it means to be successful and how best to get there. Marketers should be cautious about linking their products to generic ideas of success, like corner offices, big houses, and super-fit bodies. How can your product help a real woman achieve what she wants, not what others tell her she should want?**

● ● ● ● ● ●

Since women are much less likely than men to feel themselves following a prescribed, predetermined path to success, they are far better equipped to handle any roadblocks or interruptions that might impede their journey. In this way, women's optimism actually breeds a sort of freedom — a willingness to accept

the surprises that life brings, and to find solutions to problems that might otherwise limit their achievements.

## mind over matter

Women are often told that when they feel better they look better and vice versa, but can thinking positive thoughts actually make you physically healthier? There is solid evidence that being optimistic leads not only to better emotional health but to improved physical health, too. Consider a study involving a basketball team's ability to shoot free throws. Psychologists divided a basketball team into three groups. The first group practiced shooting free throws on the court. The second group talked about strategies for improving their free throws. The third group practiced shooting free throws — but only in their minds. When the players returned to the basketball court, the groups that had practiced — either in reality or in their minds — scored a significantly higher percentage of shots than the group that had simply talked about strategy. Perhaps most surprising, the group that had

### prescription for the future

Women would take an FDA-approved pill to . . .

- Eliminate their menstrual cycle (55%).
- Make them fit and strong, eliminating the need for exercise (54%).
- Speed up their metabolism so they could eat more without gaining weight (51%).
- Improve their confidence and self-esteem (45%).
- Make them better looking (36%).

(Source: *Health* magazine, "Women in Motion 2001")

practiced in their heads scored just as many as the group that had practiced on the court. Visualizing successful shots was every bit as valuable as physical practice. The mind prepared the body's muscles for finely tuned action without the player ever leaving his or her chair.

As I see it, every day you do one of two things: build health or produce disease in yourself.

— Adelle Davis

An unusual study of two groups of Catholic nuns gives further evidence of the close connection between the mind and physical health. Researchers at the University of Kentucky were able to obtain short autobiographies of 180 nuns from two convents in the United States, written shortly after the sisters took their final vows sometime between 1931 and 1943, when the sisters were between the ages of 18 and 32. The researchers rated each of these biographies for the amount of positive emotion and optimism a sister expressed in writing about her life. Then they compared the positive content of the autobiographies with the sisters' overall health and longevity. (The sisters all had similar socioeconomic and educational backgrounds and comparable access to health care.) The researchers found that a tendency to express positive emotions correlated very closely to a long life. The sisters who expressed the least amount of positive emotion in their early-life biographies were two and a half times more likely to have died by the year 2000 than the sisters who expressed the greatest amount of positive emotion in their autobiographies. Indeed, the sisters who expressed low levels of positive emotion died an average of ten years earlier than the sisters with highly positive emotions.

While the study of the nuns is relatively recent, the idea that attitude has a profound effect on health has been around for a long time. In 1934, J.M.T. Finney, a professor of surgery at the Johns Hopkins Medical School, announced that he would not operate on people who entered surgery believing they wouldn't survive the operation. Finney knew even then that what you expect is what you get. In the last few years, psychologists at UCLA have conducted numerous studies showing that hope and optimism are strong weapons against a wide range of diseases, including cancer. Optimists' immune systems tend to function better than those of pessimists, they heal better after heart bypass surgery, and they are more resilient in fighting HIV and AIDS.

Given the wealth of data from the Time Inc. studies showing that women are generally highly optimistic in their outlook, is it any wonder that they have a longer life expectancy than men? Here's to seeing the glass half-full!

"Hope is the thing with feathers that perches in the soul."

—Emily Dickinson

# *Trust*

As denizens of the information age, every time we answer the phone, turn on the television, read a magazine, or leave our homes, we are hit with a blizzard of opinions, sales pitches, and unsolicited advice. It is up to each of us to figure out which parts of the cacophony have meaning for our own lives and which should be dismissed as background noise. Somehow we need to decide which sources to heed and which to filter out.

We tend to gather information in several primary ways. We talk to friends. We read magazines and subscribe to e-mail alerts. We get recommendations from salespeople. We surf the Internet. And most of all, in terms of sheer quantity, we are exposed to advertising in newspapers and magazines, on TV and adorning products and places from coffee cups and phone booths to tee shirts and even the sides of buses. Barry Schwartz reports that the average American sees 3,000 ads a day. That breaks down to about 200 per waking hour, more than three per waking minute. How can we possibly process that much information? How can we decide if what we are being told is reliable or even have enough time to register all the information that is bombarding us? The answer is fairly simple — more than anything, we rely on the advice and opinions of those individuals around us who have proven themselves reliable in the past.

## who knows best?

Women were asked, "What is the most important attribute of people from whom you seek advice and information?" Their top answers were:

- They are trustworthy (95%).

- They know and understand me (83%).

- They are knowledgeable about lots of things (78%).

- They have a lifestyle similar to mine (76%).

- They talk to lots of people about lots of things (56%).

- They are an expert in a specific area (54%).

(Source: *People* magazine, "The Power of Storytelling")

## trust tops the list

*People* magazine asked women to rank the key traits that they look for in sources of advice and information. More than specific expertise or knowledge, women said they value "trustworthiness."

Women realize that a salesperson or marketer's high level of skill or expertise in a particular area doesn't necessarily make that person trustworthy. They are highly sensitive to any suggestion of a conflict of interest or hint of deception on the part of those who are advising them. This has subtle but profound implications for advertisers, as *Advertising Age* columnist Bob Garfield found when looking at a series of campaigns for Special K cereal. Several years ago, Special K's advertising featured women with perfect figures wearing cocktail dresses and preening in front of full-length mirrors. Women were invited to believe that a diet rich in Special K cereal gave these women their gorgeous bodies, but few real-world women bought into that idea. So the next campaign humorously put the language

*what she wants*
a spokesperson to relate to

Just as "a picture is worth a thousand words," people are far more likely to be influenced by a vivid interview with a single person than by the summary judgments of hundreds of people who hold the opposite point of view. In advertising, publicity, and promotion efforts, this means that even one vivid first-person account will have more impact that the most finely detailed data reports. Just as this can work to a marketer's benefit, it can also be a liability. One person's bad experience with your product, if it becomes widely known, can be more powerful than dozens of expert reports and studies to the contrary.

of body obsession into the mouths of men to reveal its irrationality and futility. Unfortunately, while that campaign won awards, it didn't sell much cereal. In its next campaign, Special K found a way to tell the truth and to sell its product. In the newer spots, we are privy to the stream-of-consciousness interior monologue of a woman waiting for a bus. She's in her mid-to-late-thirties, not too skinny but not conspicuously overweight. And, as *Advertising Age* recounts, she's obsessing: "If manufacturers could get that they could cut it to be a size 12 but they should just put a size 6 label on it, they'd sell so many more . . . . All right, where is this bus. I cannot believe I missed the bus . . . . I'm not stopping at the donut shop anymore. I mean, that's ridiculous. I'll go straight to the bakery. They ' re open early . . . . I have a treadmill . . . somewhere . . . ." Then a title card: "Don't be so hard on yourself." Garfield commended the spot, which led to increased success for the product, for acknowledging the reality of normal-looking women in their unwinnable battle against impossible standards, while declining to trot out the unattainable ideal. By speaking the truth and not promising unrealistic results, the ads earned the trust of women.

**what she wants**
someone to trust

Salespeople, managers, advertisers, and even potential dates beware! All the knowledge and experience in the world won't compensate for a perceived lack of concern for your female customer's overall satisfaction. You might be able to fool a woman once, but you'll never have the chance to do it twice. However, earn her trust and you will have a customer, client, employee—or partner!—for life.

> ## "The most called-upon prerequisite of a friend is an accessible ear."
>
> — Maya Angelou

Given this premium on trustworthiness, it makes sense that the most influential source of information or advice in a woman's life is her circle of close friends. Roper ASW has been tracking Americans' reliance on word of mouth in decision making for the past twenty-five years, and in that time, it has become an increasingly important factor. In 1977, 67% of Americans agreed that word of mouth was an important source of information and ideas for them. By 2003, a staggering 92% had come to feel that word-of-mouth was important.

Why should the opinion of an individual — even a trusted friend — be considered more valuable than the findings of an expert panel or a scientific study? Quite simply, it is because we are usually exposed to that opinion as an anecdote in a face-to-face encounter. This, in turn, makes it very easily recalled. Schwartz explains that the more available a piece of information is to memory, the more frequently we think we must have encountered it in the past.

### can we talk?

Word of mouth is the top source of information for women across three major categories:

1. Restaurants

2. Financial services

3. Cosmetics

(Source: *People* magazine, "The Power of Storytelling")

So one person's (perhaps highly atypical) opinion seems like something we ' ve heard from numerous sources and takes on the air of generally accepted truth.

Women make a habit of sharing information about products with one another. According to *People* magazine's research, most women say they have recommended a product in the past twelve months; 79% have recommended three or more products, and 57% have recommended five or more products. Women tend to communicate about most things — including

### girl power

**66%** of teenage girls say they have visited a store for the first time based solely on a friend's recommendation.

(Source: *Teen People,* "Trendspotters™")

### *what she wants*
to hear about it
through the grapevine

According to an article by Frederick F. Reichheld in the December 2003 issue of the *Harvard Business Review,* in most instances there is a strong correlation between a company's growth rate and the percentage of its customers who are promoters. If you can get women talking to each other about the value of your product or service, the sky's the limit.

products — in a storytelling style. This is a distinctively female form of communication and reflects the strong connections between women and their desire to help one another. In sharing stories, women recharge from their stressful lives, learn about themselves, and form enduring bonds. (Fewer men see the value in storytelling, and they are far less likely to view conversation as playing a critical role in their lives.) This means that when women talk about a product, their opinion will be well remembered and given real weight.

When asked to name their favorite resources for information about raising children, the Parenting Group's Mom Connection members put "other mothers" at the top of the list with health-care providers. In fact, what motivates many moms to join the panel is the chance to learn more about how their peers are navigating the waters of motherhood. "We make each other feel that we're not out of our minds," is how one focus-group mom put it.

### what she wants
### a juicy story

In advertising or promotion, look for ways to connect your product to an engaging narrative or a story line that connects to the lives and experiences of women. This will make your marketing more likely to resonate with female consumers and to be remembered by them.

## market mavens make a difference

One particular group of individuals has proven to be of real value to all shoppers, whether they are known to them personally or not. Malcolm Gladwell, in his book *The Tipping Point*, calls these people "Market Mavens." Since most shoppers don't really study and remember prices, have you ever wondered what stops unscrupulous merchants from cheating customers with meaningless promotions, or advertising sale prices that aren't really sales? Retailers know very well that a small number of people — the Market Mavens — do pay close attention to such things and that if they find something amiss they'll not only complain to management, but will go on to tell everyone they know to avoid the store. As Gladwell writes, " These are the people who keep the marketplace honest." Not only do they collect all sorts of useful information about stores and products, they are happy to share it with the rest of us. Hail to thee, Market Mavens!

All this is not to say that the media is not an important source of trusted advice in many parts of a woman's life, as can be clearly seen in the results of surveys conducted among readers of *InStyle*, dubbed "Insiders." Insiders say magazines are very potent in inspiring their fashion and beauty purchases. When they were asked what inspired their most recent fashion and/or beauty purchase, magazines ranked as a top factor — above seasonal changes and personal attention (such as salespeople or stylists) in their decision making. When it comes to home décor and entertaining, 71% of Insiders are extremely or very likely to pull out and save food or drink recipes from a magazine, 71% are extremely or very likely to read about home décor in a magazine, and 65% are extremely or very likely to watch home decoration shows on television. A *Cooking Light* survey found that 62% of women ranked magazines as their number one source of information on healthy eating habits, fitness, health, and overall well-being.

● ● ● ● ● ●

*what she wants*
stylish service with selling

Most of us have an intuitive sense of what makes a friend trustworthy. But what about a store or a business? What inspires women to feel a sense of trust for a large, faceless organization? In a few cases, trust of a particular business or brand is actually passed from one generation of consumers to the next. A study by *People en Español* found that this occurs particularly often among Hispanic women, who are far more likely than Caucasian women to purchase the same product brands that their mothers used.

● ● ● ● ● ●

The fact that magazines remain a consistently trusted source of information and advice about fashion, beauty, and home decorating products explains why retailers from Bergdorf Goodman to Abercrombie & Fitch to IKEA have taken to issuing publications that look more like magazines than catalogs. Marketers can get big results by providing strong editorial content alongside traditional product information in the materials they send to consumers.

## inspiring trust

Trend spotter and business consultant Faith Popcorn says a business can foster trust and loyalty in its female customers by being proactive, reaching out to make certain that women are satisfied with its services or products, not waiting for them to complain. In her book *EVEolution,* Popcorn explains, "Marketing is different from life. You have a well-staffed 800-number and a sexy website for her to reach you on, you say? Not good enough. That's the business equivalent of saying, 'Hey, she's got my phone number, she can call me.' If women have to go out of their way to track you down . . . if you make them jump through hoops to get service . . . if your attitude is take it or leave it . . . well, they'll leave it — and take their billions of dollars elsewhere. If she has to ask, it's too late." Ninety-six percent of female customers never complain in a store, according to Lynda Smith, a consumer-satisfaction consultant; they just never go back.

Popcorn says the way to avoid losing women customers in the first place is to adopt a strategy of "anticipatory marketing." Traditional marketing techniques — focus groups, internal company policy changes, R&D, tweaking advertising copy —are responsive; they involve putting together marketing ideas and then going out and asking consumers what they think about them. This means selling women on preconceived ideas. "Anticipating" requires having enough insight into a woman's life to fulfill her future needs without having to ask her for a blueprint. The Time Inc. Women's Group has adopted several varieties of anticipatory marketing, with gratifying results. Since teenagers' tastes and opinions change faster than most of us can fathom, to keep one step ahead, *Teen People* has enlisted the help of 14,000 "Trendspotters™." These are young adults all over the country who have signed up to report on what's in and what's out. The *Teen People* editors talk with them constantly through instant messaging and e-mail and are rewarded with a constant stream of absolutely up-to-the-minute information.

Another example of anticipatory marketing grew out of the realization that easy food preparation was a real hot-button issue for women. Thanks to magazines like *Cooking Light* and *Real Simple*, the Time Inc. Women's Group has a trove of more than 50,000 tested recipes. One-stop shopping is always a big help for the busy consumer, so the magazines teamed up with AOL and created AOL Food, an online community that allows

"It's better to put something out there and see the reaction and fix it on the fly . . . . You can't predict what's going to happen. It's another way of saying 'perfect' is the enemy of 'good enough.'"

—Meg Whitman

users to rate and review recipes, share ideas through instant
messaging and message boards, and participate in polls. Rather
than expecting users to surf countless Web sites for recipes and
recommendations, Time Inc. was able to take its knowledge of
what was important to them and provide an invaluable online
resource. And it was a hit!

For retailers, anticipatory marketing includes taking the
needs of women into account when designing the physical
shopping environment, adapting it to reflect the desires of
women customers, not waiting for women to identify problems or
trouble spots. Remember, if a woman has an unhappy experience in a
store, she is far more likely simply to go somewhere else next time rather than to
complain to the merchant.

### what she wants
consistent quality

Brand extensions can be perilous if they lead to giving consumers too many choices, but they can be truly lethal if the new products are not of the same quality or value as the original. Every product bearing the brand's name must be as worthy of a consumer's trust as the original. Watering down a strong brand with under-performing sidelines can make consumers give up on the whole product line in a flash. When working on a brand personality, it is important to remember the words of advice that apply so well to people: "Be yourself" and "Don't try to be someone you're not."

# "Follow your hunches. They're usually based on facts filed away just below the conscious level. "

— Dr. Joyce Brothers

The GMDC offers its members five specific strategies for satisfying the needs of women shoppers and cementing the bond of trust with them. They recommend the following:

● ● ● ● ● ●

*what she wants*
whatever is next

Marketers need to operate like detectives, searching for the clues that reveal new consumer patterns and tastes. Those clues provide the insights that keep you on top in market share. For example, the magazines of Time Inc. are constantly putting researchers in the field and conducting grassroots interviews, focus groups, and surveys. Kristin van Ogtrop, managing editor of *Real Simple,* says that doing this helps editors know how readers are responding to specific stories and keep their fingers on the collective pulse of their particular audience.

● ● ● ● ● ●

1. **Female-Friendly Environment:** Products, categories, and stores must all have the "right" environment. From ambience and fixtures, to lighting and product adjacencies, shopping must be comfortable for women.

2. **The Fast Lane:** Women want both a streamlined shopping experience and a wide range of services to save their time. This is about both one-stop shopping and being able to do more in less time in the store.

3. **Information, Please:** Women feel that most retailers do not adequately provide helpful and meaningful information about nutrition, health conditions, and women's issues. Be the one who does!

4. **Life-Stage Solutions:** A woman's interest in health and well-being is often triggered by a life-stage event such as childbirth, menopause, a chronic health condition, aging, or illness. Display and group products accordingly.

5. **Stolen Moments:** Finding a few stolen moments of time to engage in personal activities and relaxation is often at the core of a woman's overall sense of well-being. A sense of being pampered or nurtured, no matter how small, will be appreciated.

(Source: GMDC, "Women's Well-Being Merchandising Strategies")

## one good truth deserves another

Virginia Woolf once wrote, "If you do not tell the truth about yourself, you cannot tell it about other people." It's a sentiment that resonates with many women today.

Just as most women value trustworthiness in others, it's a trait they make every effort to embody in their own lives. The *Real Simple* success study found that 85% of women who consider themselves "very successful" also describe themselves as "ethical." Much in the way today's women define success along emotional axes rather than material ones, here the study shows that they tend to attribute their achievements to traits of character as much as to specific technical skills. Knowing that she is part of a network of trustworthy advice givers and information sharers provides a woman the ultimate security. In her book *When the Canary Stops Singing: Women's Perspectives on Transforming Business,* Pat Barrentine reminds readers of the old custom of taking canaries into coal mines, using the birds as a signal to the miners that the air had become toxic. When the canaries stopped singing, the miners knew it was time to get out. With the circles of trust they forge with their friends, women have found a reliable "canary" to tell them when something's not right — long before they stop singing themselves.

"If we could sell our experiences for what they cost us, we'd all be millionaires."

—Abigail Van Buren

# *Expression*

Once upon a time, the search for the best in style and design required a visit to the high priests of chic on Madison Avenue or Rodeo Drive. But today, style is in evidence all around us. It is in the earthy tones and sculpted counters of your neighborhood Starbucks and in the simple sleekness of the iPod tucked in your hip pocket. It is available coast-to-coast and at all price points thanks to Target product lines by design gurus like Michael Graves and Isaac Mizrahi. In every room of the house, in every house on the block, our most mundane items — from potato peelers to alarm clocks — are routinely engineered to be as aesthetically pleasing as they are useful. Style has infused our world, permeated our culture, and become an everyday experience. *Time* magazine has dubbed the first ten years of the twenty-first century the Decade of Design, declaring that "Americans are likely to appreciate style when they see it and demand it when they don't."

Along with this tidal wave of style, we ' re seeing bold new patterns in consumer behavior, something DYG Inc. calls "cultural cocktailing." Their research shows that two-thirds of women today say they "go their own way" when making style choices. Cultural cocktailing is a blending of a variety of beliefs and behaviors that never went together before. For example, it's easy to imagine a woman today who is a platinum V.I.P. card-holder at Saks Fifth Avenue and also shops weekly at Costco. This is what professor and author Sharon Zukin calls "reverse aspirational shopping." Typically, women used to shop slightly above their station in life. Now they tend to shop for the lowest price on commodities — so they can afford the luxuries they really want. Mikki Taylor, Beauty Director and Cover Editor of *Essence* magazine, says that this is especially true of African-American women. According to the *Essence* " Window on Our Women Report," 50% of African-American women agree that they like to look good regardless of what it costs, compared with 28% of women in the general marketplace.

**what she wants**
thoughtfully designed
products and stores

Ann Moore, C.E.O. of Time Inc., points out that when you are launching a product in the American marketplace you just can't get away with shoddy or poor design anymore. Good design of products and stores is helping to fuel the shopping revolution. With a Gap on every corner and a Pottery Barn catalog in every mailbox, everyone knows and expects good design. This means you can't afford to cut corners when it comes to your logo, your packaging, or your display materials.

# "Fashions fades; style is eternal."

### —Yves Saint Laurent

A woman's style is not typically a constant thing, but rather something that evolves over time and that can be a source of fun and experimentation. *InStyle*'s research shows that it is quite common for women to experiment with their personal style or to purchase items of a style different than their own. Three-quarters or more say they often or sometimes experiment with their fashion (86%), hair (74%), or makeup (75%) style, or even their home décor style (72%). Many also like to purchase items that are not in their typical style just to try things out.

## gotta be me

Eight out of ten *InStyle* Insiders think it is extremely or very important to reflect their personal style when purchasing fashion and beauty items (**84%** and **81%**, respectively).

Many Insiders also think it is extremely or very important to reflect their personal style in their home décor and entertaining (**76%**, **64%**).

(Source: *InStyle* magazine, "Inside Style")

5

## a trendsetter for every occasion

Where do women get new ideas about style? Whether they care to admit it or not, Meg Ryan's hairstyle in the 1990s and Carrie Bradshaw's fashion and drink choices in 2000 made a huge impact on women's style purchases nationwide. Of course, most women aren't slavishly following a celebrity's style, but rather using it as a source of inspiration in creating and personalizing their own style.

*what she wants*
to experiment with style

Women's interest in experimenting with style gives marketers a great way to introduce them to an entire line of connected products. Redecorating an entire room may seem daunting, so how about trying some new throw pillows? And then perhaps a coordinating window treatment? And a pair of lamps from the same designer? Encourage a trial purchase for fun, and show how that one item can be built upon with other items over time. The same strategy makes sense for hair, makeup, and fashion lines. And women's desire to change it up doesn't stop with shopping. Whether it is an outing with friends or family, a day with the kids, or in dating situations, trying out a new routine, restaurant, or activity is a great way to energize any woman.

No longer do women have to follow the latest fads to feel stylish. In the past, sporting the latest trendy item or look signified being a part of a group, which gave social reassurance and comfort. Think June Cleaver dresses in the 1950s, flip hairstyles in the 1960s, and shoulder-padded power suits in the 1980s. Now, women are more likely to see style as a means to express their own individuality. They are not limited in their style choices; they can be natural, sexy, and sophisticated, all in one day or on many different occasions. For example, Insiders make a distinction between their preferred weekend and weekday fashion and beauty styles. For the workweek, Insiders will likely be sporting a classic look both in terms of their fashion (41%) and beauty (41%) styles. On the weekends, however, Insiders opt for a look that is more natural (22% fashion, 31% beauty).

## the way you look tonight

Celebrities are an important source of style inspiration for Insiders.

**91%** say they have been inspired by a celebrity's style.

**79%** say reading about how celebrities create their own sense of style helps them in shaping their own sense of style.

**73%** feel better about their style if they see that a celebrity has a similar item of clothing or uses the same makeup product as they do.

(Source: *InStyle* magazine, "Inside Style")

# 5

## "Remember that you have not only the right to be an individual, you have an obligation to be one."

—Eleanor Roosevelt

### the feel-good factor

Style used to be about collection — filling a closet or an entire house with items that had been decreed "desirable." Today, there's an emotional connection with style — it's the thing that moves women to buy. Purchases are less about conspicuous consumption or keeping up with the Joneses and more about how they make women feel, the emotional reward. When Insiders were asked what prompted their fashion, beauty, and home décor purchases other than necessary updates, "I just needed a change" ranked number one across the board. Many style changes are triggered by changes in emotions, the way someone feels after she has received a promotion or ended a relationship or lost a few pounds. In their book *Trading Up*, Michael Silverstein and Neil Fiske put it this way: "For many consumers, especially women, buying luxuries is no longer a guilty self-indulgence; it is their right and even their obligation to make sure they are feeling their best." A luxury purchase does not necessarily have to involve a big-ticket item, like major jewelry or a new car, to be emotionally satisfying for these women. Even something as simple as choosing a premium priced shampoo over her usual brand can deliver momentary feelings of comfort and well-being.

## shoes, glorious shoes

In the realm of fashion, "shoes" is the category that the largest number of Insiders say they are most passionate about (36%), they enjoy shopping for the most (36%), and they tend to splurge on the most (34%).

(Source: *InStyle* magazine, "Inside Style")

**5** ● ●

The *Real Simple* success study found that American women today are doing an interesting "two-step" when it comes to linking materialism and success. On the one hand, they adamantly refuse to associate success directly with wealth, fame, or "stuff." While abstract ideas like "happiness" and "peace of mind" are at the top of the list of words that best capture their view of success, at the very bottom of that list are wealth (15%), power (15%), prestige (14%), and fame (7%). As a woman from Boston put it: "If I'm successful, first of all, it comes from here. It's got to feel good inside. I don't think of success as monetary." Yet, while women say they do not personally believe in equating material wealth with success, almost nine in ten believe that "society" defines success in "very materialistic terms." This does not mean that women are

● ● ● ● ● ● ●

### what she wants
#### products that make her feel good

What is the emotional message of your product? As important as technical specifications and detailed facts are in making a product worth purchasing, the thing that most consumers will take away from advertising and promotion campaigns is the way the idea of the product makes them feel. That is what will drive the purchase. Then, the level of satisfaction the product actually delivers will determine if you have found a repeat customer.

● ● ● ● ● ● ●

# "My recipe for life is not being afraid of myself, afraid of what I think, or of my opinions"

### – Eartha Kitt

resisting luxury. On the contrary, from 1999 to 2003 luxury spending in the United States grew four times faster than overall spending. But, according to a *Real Simple* study of women's attitudes toward luxury, 80% of those buying high-end products said that the driving considerations behind these purchases were quality and value. Only 4% cited concerns about status and prestige as relevant. On the whole, African-American women are more likely to say that owning luxury or upscale products makes them feel better about themselves: 42% as compared to 26% of the general marketplace, according to *Essence*'s "Window on Our Women Report."

**⑤** ● ●

## paradox of materialism

Most of these women firmly believe that success is all about self-expression, not about meeting someone else's standards. "Success can be defined however you would like to define it, whatever it is that makes you content, and not necessarily what anybody else might think is success," explained a woman in North Carolina during a *Real Simple* focus group, articulating a widely held view. Indeed, 84% of the women who participated in the success study agreed that the definition of success is

● ● ● ● ● ● ●

*what she wants*
a woman's right to luxury

Luxury purchases are often viewed as the "treats" women give themselves while they are working at raising happy children, finding an enjoyable career, growing intellectually, and sustaining good relationships. Today's successful women are perfectly happy to spend money on themselves, their homes, and their families, but they are much more likely to do so when the product speaks to the new definition of success

● ● ● ● ● ● ●

something for each individual woman to determine on her own. (Only 14% felt there are generally agreed-upon standards of success.) Interestingly, this opinion is held equally across all demographics. No matter if they are married or single, if they have children or do not, if they are employed outside the home or not, if they have a household income of less than $50,000 or more than $150,000, eight in ten women agree that success is best considered as something personal, individual, and self-defined.

*what she wants*
quality over status

When it comes to luxury product and service marketing, a new kind of positioning that takes the "Paradox of Materialism" into account is likely to be more effective. Remember, your consumers do not see success as being about making money and accumulating fabulous possessions; money and things are not seen as ends in themselves as they used to be. The buyer considers luxury purchases worthwhile because of their high quality and value, not because they confer automatic status.

This study suggests the emergence of a phenomenon that might be thought of as the "Paradox of Materialism." Women do acknowledge that money cannot be entirely divorced from success: 82% say that having money helps one achieve success in life, and 76% wish they had more money. Furthermore, they openly enjoy the pleasures that money provides — the majority of women in the study express an interest in activities like traveling, home decorating and improvement, and treating themselves at a spa. But the underlying reality is that women do not consider money as the end goal of success, but as one of its by-products. It is a subtle but crucial distinction: being successful is not the same thing as getting rich. Rather, being successful (that is, having happy children, an enjoyable career, an inviting home, etc.) allows women to feel more free to enjoy the accompanying pleasures of financial security and to treat themselves on occasion. The satisfactions of having money are recast as rewards for fulfilling the internal, emotional

aspects of success. For example, in creating the "comfortable, inviting home" that is one of the cornerstones of the new definition of success, women today can simultaneously embrace the things that money can buy, express their personal taste, and avoid the dissonance of engaging in conspicuous consumption or self-indulgence. Research conducted by the Parenting Group found that for mothers, financial success is above all about ensuring a secure future, with investing and saving for education as closely linked priorities. The Mom Connection revealed that the majority of moms are not concerned with "keeping up with the Joneses," but rather with maintaining the same lifestyle they enjoyed before they had children.

"If I had known what it would be like to have it all, I might have been willing to settle for less."

—Lily Tomlin

Women today express their individuality through their style and fashion choices, but also in far more subtle, interior ways. In a world where style has become an integral part of almost every commodity, it is interesting to see so many women using the choices they are offered as vehicles for creating their own distinctive look. As luxury purchases have become fueled less by concerns about status and more by personal satisfaction, so women's definitions of success have shifted from exterior symbols to interior peace of mind. The days of "one size fits all" are gone for good.

# "If you want the girl next door, go next door."
## —Joan Crawford

# *Control*

Remember the old advertising jingle, "Have it your way…"? That could be the theme song of many women today. To put it simply, they want control over the products they are buying. For manufacturers the meaning is clear. People will flock to businesses that view them as participants in the process rather than just customers. There are examples all around us. People love *American Idol* because it puts them in charge — they get to vote at the end of the show. Customized rings for cell phones have become a multibillion dollar business. According to *Time* magazine, Apple sold more than 50 million downloads on its iTunes service in its first year alone. Music lovers no longer want the whole 16-song CD — they want to create their own playlists of songs and listen to them whenever and wherever they choose. Digital video recorders (DVRs) like TiVo allow television viewers to avoid advertising and promotion and see only what they

**⑥** ● ●

want to see. DVRs, cable on demand, and satellite services give consumers access to countless programs and films on their own personal time schedules.

This raises an interesting question. Does this desire for control over the little things suggest that people are feeling a lack of control over the larger issues in their lives? Would we be as insistent on having a dozen choices of bottled water if we weren't feeling a little bit at sea about big-picture problems? We all want to control the controllable. A woman at a *Real Simple* focus group said it well: "I may not be able to control the Taliban, but at least I can get dinner on the table."

### women's worries

What are the biggest concerns on women's minds?
- Financial security **(47%)**
- Children **(30%)**
- Physical health **(27%)**
- Relationship with spouse/partner **(27%)**
- Emotional well-being **(16%)**
- Aging parents **(9%)**
- My own aging **(9%)**
- Education **(9%)**
- Career **(9%)**
- Appearance **(4%)**

(Source: *Health* magazine, "Women in Motion 2003")

# "Genius is an infinite capacity for taking life by the scruff of the neck."

**—Katharine Hepburn**

Women are looking to control a wide range of things, some tangible, some more esoteric: their appearance, their finances, their weight, their schedules, their emotions. Unfortunately, all too often, they feel that the marketplace is not helping them to achieve this in some of the most basic areas. Fashion may seem like a category where women are offered more than enough choices to guarantee they can get what they want, but the truth is that the vast majority of women don't feel that the options available to them are satisfactory on the most basic level. For example, 92% of women surveyed by *InStyle* said that "finding flattering clothing for my body type" is important, yet only 25% were satisfied with their options in this area, a huge gap in satisfaction. Similarly, 72% think it's important to find stylish items that are comfortable, but just 26% are currently satisfied with what they are offered to purchase. Every clothing designer and retailer should keep one startling fact in mind: on *Real Simple*'s Problem Detector list, the ninth most commonly cited problem — out of everything women face in their lives — is, "I have trouble finding pants that fit." If universal health care is beyond us, can't we at least get some well-tailored pants off the rack?

## money matters

As compared with Caucasian women, African-American women are:

- More likely to be the primary decision maker for major household purchases.

- More aspirational—two times as likely to say getting as much education as possible, owning their own business, and having the latest technology are very or extremely important.

(Source: *Essence* magazine, "Window on Our Women Report")

When it comes to money, *Health* magazine found that women have greater control over the financial decisions of their households than might have been popularly supposed. According to their research, 86% of women are either the main decision makers (32%) or joint decision makers (54%) of household financial matters. Eighty-two percent of women are actively investing, 76% are comfortable making important financial decisions, and 69% are saving for retirement. As we saw in areas of optimism and self-confidence, African-American women are taking the lead in matters of personal and family finance as well. They are making the important decision to invest in their own future success.

● ● ● ● ● ●

*what she wants*
specific, realistic products and solutions

*Real Simple* found that women who consider themselves to be "very successful" are the same women who habitually make checklists and set specific goals for themselves. These women will be highly receptive to products and services that offer them practical, achievable solutions to the organizational and logistical challenges of their daily lives. Vague promises won't appeal to them as much as specific strategies for success.

● ● ● ● ● ●

# 6 ● ●

# "A woman is like a tea bag: you never know her strength until you drop her in hot water."

## —Nancy Reagan

Allowing women — and men, for that matter — to have more control over the way they do their jobs can contribute greatly to an organization's success. In *Toxic Work*, Barbara Reinhold explains, "the kind of control that comes with narrowly defined jobs is disastrous in our volatile information and service economy. Research shows clearly that the control we need now can only come from inviting workers to be more autonomous, helping to shape and reshape their own jobs in response to rapid market changes." The very best managers give their employees a clear sense of direction but do not hand down specific instructions on "how to get there." Rather, they encourage them to design their own work. This can lead to par-

ticularly impressive results with women, whose minds are especially well suited to finding unexpected and even unconventional solutions to workplace challenges.

## women who think too much

Generally speaking, feeling in control is a good and empowering thing, but in her book *Women Who Think Too Much*, Susan Nolen-Hoeksema points out the danger that can come from women wanting too much control too often. She warns that women, more than men, have a tendency to ruminate about anything and everything — their appearance, their family, their career, their health — and that they often feel this is just part of being a woman, a reflection of their feminine, caring, self-aware nature.

"The past cannot be changed. The future is yet in your power."
—Mary Pickford

This may be partly true, but over-thinking issues that are beyond their control can also lead to problems for women. She encourages women to find ways to be the "directors" of their own emotional lives, to avoid the trap of blaming themselves for events they cannot control or alter.

Feeling in control without worrying about things that are beyond one's sphere of influence can be accompanied by a range of important health benefits. Conversely, researchers have found that the people most likely to have heart disease are those whose jobs make high demands while granting very little autonomy. Reinhold underlines this complex interconnection of physical and emotional health when she says, "the worst thing that can happen to workers, in terms of both productivity and health, is to have high demands (which almost all workers do these days) but low control over how they meet those demands. "

## crunch time

Though **70%** of women "are not passionate about" exercising, **77%** do it at least two times per month, citing these top three reasons:

- Manage weight

- Reduce stress

- Reduce health problems

(Source: *Health* magazine, "Women in Motion 2003")

A study conducted in Sweden sheds some more light on the physical side effects of feeling in control. It compared the experiences of two groups of regular suburban commuters on a morning train ride. The study found that riders who boarded the train 79 minutes from Stockholm experienced much less stress, as measured by increases in their adrenaline levels, than commuters who had only a 43-minute ride. Why should the longer commute be less stressful? Because the group who boarded earlier found themselves on an empty train, they had far greater control over where and with whom they sat, as well as where to place their briefcases and other bags. Meanwhile, commuters who boarded a fairly crowded train farther down the line experienced much less choice and control over their experience. Research by psychologist Martin Seligman, author of *Learned Optimism,* suggests that the more control people have, the less helpless and thus the less depressed they will be.

## our bodies, ourselves

Another area where women desire a level of control is in issues related to their health and well-being. Women make three-fourths of the health care decisions in American households and spend nearly two out of every three U.S. health care dollars, approximately $500 billion each year. Women account for 61% of physician visits, purchase 59% of all prescriptions, and account for two-thirds of all hospital procedures. The Internet has turned out to be a hugely important resource in terms of women getting the information they need to take more personal control over health-related issues. According to a 2000 Harris Poll, two-thirds of all online health-site users in North America today are female.

### don't go changin'

If women could change one thing about their appearance, and money was not a consideration, they would choose:

- Dental whitening **(66%)**
- Braces/dental cosmetic surgery **(44%)**
- Laser eye surgery **(41%)**
- Tummy tuck **(40%)**
- Liposuction **(30%)**
- Breast surgery **(25%)**
- Eye lift **(19%)**
- Chemical peel **(16%)**
- Face lift **(16%)**
- Nose job **(8%)**
- Botox/collagen injections **(8%)**

(Source: *Health* magazine, "Women in Motion 2001")

# "The kind of beauty I want most is the hard-to-get kind that comes from within — strength, courage, dignity."

**—Ruby Dee**

It may be hard to believe, but until quite recently there was some doubt about whether America's obsession with healthy living was a passing, regional fad or a broader trend that would take hold nationally. In the mid-1980s, *Southern Living* magazine began running a very popular column called *Healthy Living.* With the publisher's fingers crossed, that successful column was spun off into a new monthly magazine called *Cooking Light.* Now, seventeen years after its launch, *Cooking Light* has emerged as the largest food and fitness magazine in the country, surely putting to rest any notion that issues of health and well-being are of interest to only a small group of consumers. *Cooking Light'*s research underscores the connection between issues of health and feeling in control: Their studies found that 43% of women agree that "taking measures to live a healthy lifestyle is a way for me to personally control my life and my future."

*People* has run more than twenty-five covers about diet and weight in recent years, and they have found that these issues typically have newsstand sales 7% higher than the average. Another example of the ongoing quest to have more control over our health and well-being is found in the ever-increasing numbers of Americans practicing yoga over the last decade:

**Yoga Participants (in millions)**
- 1990: 4.0
- 1994: 6.0
- 1998: 18.0
- 2002: 28.0

(Source: *Yoga Journal*)

Surely many of these new yoga practitioners would agree with a study recently conducted by *Cooking Light* magazine. It found that 74% of all women believe that "small, healthy improvements in lifestyle today can lead to big benefits later."

Feeling in control is integral to a woman's overall sense of well-being, extending far beyond her psychological health and directly affecting many aspects of her physical health. We live in a hectic and often confusing world where much seems beyond our control, so it is little wonder that women are looking for practical help in areas of their lives where they can exert real influence.

From health to finances to fashion, they are actively seeking strategies and solutions that provide high levels of satisfaction and control. In providing these solutions, marketers and retailers are helping women to lead infinitely healthier and happier lives.

# *Connections*

If the 1970s was famously dubbed the "me" decade, it seems likely that the 2000s might someday be thought of as the "we" decade. Women, in particular, are feeling an acute desire to reconnect with one another, seeking ways to engage with each other on a regular basis. Whether this is a result of post-9/11 anxiety or some other less specific cause, surveys show women attaching more and more importance to interpersonal connections. *Real Simple*'s Problem Detector research finds that "more than ever, people want community." In fact, the task of keeping in touch with friends and family as much as they'd like surged from #17 to #7 on the Problem Detector survey between 2001 and 2002. Similarly, the Parenting Group has seen a notable increase in concern among mothers about having enough time to spend with their female friends. The percentage of moms worried about this jumped from 66% in 1999 to 76% in 2003.

## baby, we were born to talk

Scientific evidence supports the idea that human beings are biologically and psychologically constructed to connect with one another. Psychologist Kathleen Brehony suggests that we think of the explosive growth and development in a human's first three years of life as a sort of "map-drawing process." This early map will guide us for the rest of our lives as we make our way in the world. She writes, "What is increasingly clear is that love and connection are the cartographers — the forces that draw the map . . . . Attachment is a basic human need deeply rooted in millions of years of species evolution. Quickly connecting to caregivers is essential if we are to develop as full human beings. We 're biologically hardwired to ripen through loving, secure experiences with caregivers." Compared with other species, human beings are born premature and must continue to develop outside the womb — more than 75% of the human brain develops only after birth.

## "Trouble shared is trouble halved."
### — Dorothy Sayers

While this predisposition for early connection is true of all humans, biological differences between the sexes make adult women more likely than men to feel the urge to seek close connections with others. When researchers at UCLA studied the differences in how men and women react to stress, they found that when women feel stressed, they respond with a surge of brain chemicals, such as oxytocin, that produce a feeling of calm and make them want to seek one another's company. (Oxytocin is the same biochemical that promotes maternal behavior.) Once a woman engages in connecting or befriending behaviors, even more oxytocin is released into her body, which leads to a desire for even more social contact, which in turns leads to greater relaxation. It seems that estrogen in women enhances the effects of oxytocin, while testosterone in men reduces its effects.

# "It's the friends you call up at 4 a.m. that matter. "

— Marlene Dietrich

Harvard professor Carol Gilligan points out that the tendency in females to connect starts very early. "People used to look out on the playground and say that the boys were playing soccer and the girls were doing nothing," she notes. "But the girls weren't doing nothing — they were talking. They were talking about the world to one another. And they became very expert about that in a way the boys did not."

There is strong evidence that women are trained from childhood to pay more attention to their emotions than men are. Research by developmental psychologists at Stanford University and the Institute of Psychology in London has found a major difference in the ways parents treat their daughters and sons: they tend to recognize and support expressions of sadness and anxiety in girls, but they discourage similar emotions in boys. Inevitably, such early lessons can have a lifelong impact on the ways men and women handle emotionally difficult times and on the places they look for help and support.

### better than sex?

Conversation is so primal for women that they find it better than sex for relieving stress.

Over half **(53%)** of women say that talking with close friends or family members helps "a lot" when they feel stressed, while only **17%** say sex helps "a lot."

Men find talking and sex to be similarly helpful when feeling stressed (**36%** and **35%,** respectively).

(Source: *People* magazine, "The Power of Storytelling")

"Let us make a special effort to stop communicating with each other, so we can have some conversation."

—Judith Martin

### home is where the hive is

Perhaps some of these traditional gender-based differences in behavior will blur as American society's rules and values keep evolving. For example, consider how our connotations of the word "home" have changed over the last twenty years. In the 1980s, the home was often seen as a reflection of one's own status. In the 1990s, it was a private haven for the family from

> "It's fun to get together and have something good to eat at least once a day. That's what human life is all about."

— Julia Child

a fast-moving outside world. Now, in the 2000s, it serves as the emotional center for connecting with family and friends. Roper has found that Americans' tendency to describe their home as a social hub — a place where they often socialize with others— is up 14% since 1998. "Cocooning" was the 1990s term frequently used to describe America's retreat back inside the home. It was all about keeping your family safe by focusing on each other and not letting others in. "Hiving," the phrase used to describe what is going on today, is about having a home that is abuzz with social engagement. It's about inviting others in, entertaining — home is a place for fun and enjoyment. Mary Catherine Bateson points out that the word "home" has many layers of meaning — we "keep" a house but we "make" a home. It's an act of creation, of building. More than ever, we are creating and sustaining our homes in new ways, discovering emotional links between the abstract idea of "home" and the material things it contains. As Bateson says, "The homes we create for ourselves are far more than physical shelters; the homeless lack far more than homes . . . . Rooms and apartments foster human relationships within and around them."

## talking points

. . . . . . . . . . . . . . . . . . . . . . . . . . . . . . . . . . . . . . . . . . . . . .

Conversation serves many purposes in women's lives.

### Recharging

*"Having a good conversation with a friend helps me re-charge my battery."*

- **71%** of women agree, **49%** of men agree.

*"I sometimes need to talk about what's going on in my life just to vent my feelings or frustrations."*

- **54%** of women agree, **34%** of men agree.

### Validation

*"When other people tell me about their problems I often realize that my life isn't so bad."*

- **60%** of women agree, **50%** of men agree.

### Learning

*"I learn a lot from hearing stories about what's going on in other people's lives."*

- **41%** of women agree, **34%** of men agree.

(Source: People magazine, "The Power of Storytelling")

. . . . . . . . . . . . . . . . . . . . . . . . . . . . . . . . . . . . . . . . . . . . . .

*InStyle* Insiders are proof of this: they are entertaining in their home or at a friend's house three times a month on average. This entertaining takes many forms. They are planning dinner parties, theme parties, and parties for more than twenty-five people. Seventeen percent even said they are extremely or very likely to take a cooking class this year. Fifty-six percent say they splurge on specialty food items when entertaining, and they are just as likely to buy an expensive bottle of wine if the occasion presents itself as they are a bottle for under $15. According to *Cooking Light*'s research, 42% of women entertain friends or relations at home once a month or more.

All this "hiving" serves a multitude of purposes, including putting us back in touch with ourselves. Pulitzer Prize–winning journalist Anna Quindlen says, "I only really understand myself, what I'm really thinking and feeling, when I've talked it over with my circle of female friends. When days go by without that connection, I feel like a radio playing in an empty room."

## wired women

- **63%** of women have access to the Internet.
- **62%** buy things online more than once a year.
- **39%** say their recent tech purchase was to benefit the whole family.
- **34%** say their recent tech purchase was to benefit themselves.

(Source: *Health* magazine, "Women in Motion 2001")

## evolving connections

One of the ways that increasing numbers of women are finding to connect with each other is the Internet. Women make up more than half of the online population, and the numbers are rising quickly — especially among women over age 55. In the early days of the Internet boom, many trend watchers predicted that women, as a group, would not be big users of the Internet due to a "lack of affinity" or an innate mistrust of technology. Such predictions were way off the mark; women are extremely comfortable with the Inter-

*what she wants*
short, sweet breaks

When creating online marketing campaigns, don't forget that time is a valuable commodity for women. As reported in *Advertising Age*, when Chrysler launched a very successful online game geared toward women to help Web visitors "determine their travel personality and uncover which of the automaker's vehicles suited their profile," most women engaged with the test for 7.6 minutes. This was no accident, according to Mike Vann of YaYa Media, which created the game. "Women are busy," Vann said. "We didn't want to lose them because the game was too long. We didn't want the game play to go over ten minutes." Also, while men are typically drawn to online games emphasizing competition and action, women prefer card, puzzle, and words games that promote self-fulfillment and community.

net, discovering in it a vehicle for limitless connection. According to a 2004 study conducted by Digital Marketing Services as reported in *Advertising Age*, women over 40 spend more hours per week playing online games than men do — nine hours compared with six hours. And 28% of them play games between midnight and 5 a.m. — a reflection of their stressful, over-full days.

Women are not using their time online for idle chat.Data from the 2002 Pew Internet and American Life study reveals that after a year of accessing the Internet, as users become comfortable with communicating online, their use of e-mail gets more serious and important. As the sense of newness diminishes, random notes to friends and family decrease. In their place, e-mails sharing real news and concerns or seeking advice from friends and family significantly increase. More than 84% of e-mailers say they use online service to keep in contact with family members and 80% use it to keep in touch with

> "When you are a mother, you are never really alone in your thoughts.  A mother always has to think twice, once for herself and once for her child."
>
> —Sophia Loren

friends. Women, in particular, say they value the Internet because it strengthens their bonds with others. Sixty percent of women claim that the Internet has improved their connection to parents, siblings, and children.

Of course, there are lots of other ways to communicate besides the Internet these days, and a study conducted by the Parenting Group showed that many mothers today are making use of all the means at their disposal. Over 90% of women surveyed felt that new options such as cell phones and text messaging made it "easier to keep track of friends and family" and helped them to "feel more connected." Nearly 80% of moms said they rely more heavily on communications devices now than they did before they had kids, and two-thirds of moms reported they were more willing to try new sorts of communication devices now than they were before they had kids. Beyond technology, moms still stay connected with their kids by reading books, eating dinner together, and shopping with them. The more things change . . . .

### what she wants
### a sense of community

African-American and Hispanic women's strong sense of community has a direct impact on many of their habits as consumers. They are more likely than Caucasian women to purchase their hair-care products at salons, which they visit more frequently. Thirty-six percent of African-American women visit a hair salon or beauty shop once every two to three weeks, compared to 5% of General Market women, according to the *Essence* magazine "Window on Our Women Report."

## the power of word of mouth

Women's predisposition to connect has important implications for the marketplace. They consistently enjoy talking about products, recommending specific items to one another that provide satisfaction. And, as we've seen, these recommendations are considered highly trustworthy. Since they typically come in the form of a personal story or anecdote, they are far more likely to be remembered than any form of advertising or marketing.

Product recommendations are particularly widespread in minority communities. For many African-American women, beauty salons are a frequent destination and come to function almost like community centers — places where news is exchanged, advice is shared, and friendships are formed and strengthened.

## "Perhaps the most important thing we ever give each other is our attention."
### —Rachel Naomi Remen

## what's the buzz?

What are women talking about?

- **91%** What's going on in friends' or family's lives
- **91%** Current events
- **80%** Work
- **78%** Products

(Source: *People* magazine, "The Power of Storytelling")

In his best-selling book *The Tipping Point*, Malcolm Gladwell suggests the special role women play in building buzz when he explains how a novel with little advertising, a relatively unknown author, and few reviews became a fixture on best-seller lists and sold 2.5 million copies. The novel—*Divine Secrets of the Ya-Ya Sisterhood* by Rebecca Wells — was discovered and embraced by a handful of women's book-groups in the San Francisco Bay Area a year after it was first published. Because *Ya-Ya* was read, loved, and discussed in groups, it became a social experience that women cherished and wanted to be able to talk about with their friends and family. From group to group, word spread like a literary epidemic from a few dozen passionate women to a nationwide audience of millions. Wells had a huge bestseller, but the women also benefited; as Wells noted when meeting with groups of her fans, "I began to realize that these women had built their own Ya-Ya relationships, not so much to the book but to each other." In other words, sharing information about products is at its heart an important way that women strengthen their bonds of friendship and trust. Retailers and manufacturers are the lucky co-beneficiaries of this phenomenon.

As this research suggests, women are more likely than men to define themselves in terms of their relationships and to maintain social networks that are broader and deeper than men's. Harvard sociologist Ron Kessler has found that, as a result of these tendencies, women are also more likely than men to feel affected by traumatic events in the lives of others. When a friend or family member is facing illness or some other major problem, women are more likely than men to suffer from symptoms of depression.

## the teenage connection

At home, teens take most responsibility for:

- Household chores **(73%)**
- Family purchases **(55%)**
- Family social plans **(34%)**
- Meal preparation **(34%)**
- Taking care of siblings **(33%)**
- Being family "tech guru" **(29%)**
- Food purchases **(26%)**
- Family vacation plans **(23%)**

(Source: *Teen People*, "Trendspotters™")

# "Cherish your human connections: your relationships with friends and family."

— Barbara Bush

Forging social connections takes time; getting to know someone intimately is a long process. As Barry Schwartz notes, "Only in Hollywood do such attachments come instantly and effortlessly." In the real world, it would seem to require lots of free time and a relatively flexible schedule to share the daily ups and downs of a friend without feeling an increase in stress and distraction in one's own life. And, as we saw in chapter 2, time is something that women do not have in surplus.

## where did the family time go?

On a practical level, a lack of time does affect our ability today to connect as much as we would like with others in our social circle, and even with the people who share our own homes. This problem starts early. According to a national survey conducted by the University of Michigan, since the late 1970s American children's daily schedules and activities have undergone a major change: Over that time, the average child has lost twelve hours a week in free time, including a 25% drop in playing and a 50% drop in nonorganized outdoor activities. According to the same survey, conversation between parents and children — time spent just talking — has almost entirely disappeared, and there has been a 28% decline in the number of family vacations. Other national surveys have found a one-third decrease in the number of families who say they have dinner together regularly.

### help others, help yourself

**48%** of women participate in community or civic groups/causes throughout the year.

(Source: *Cooking Light*, "*Cooking Light* Insight")

Dr. William J. Doherty and Barbara Z. Carlson, in their book *Putting Family First*, report that the National Association of Elementary School Principals is now tackling the problem of overscheduled children. The association recommends that

young children become involved in only one extracurricular activity at a time, with that activity meeting no more than once or twice a week. A national poll of teenagers funded by the White House in spring 2000 found that over one-fifth of American teens rated "not having enough time with parents" as their top worry, a percentage that tied for first place with "getting a good education." Despite these concerns, teens do exercise considerable influence in their households. According to a *Teen People* survey, 93% of teens have some sort of responsibility at home — with more than half saying they manage household chores and influence family purchases.

## get connected, get healthy

Even though it's time-consuming and many of us are having trouble doing it, having close social relationships seems to be the single most important factor in making us happy. Schwartz says, "People who are married, who have good friends, and who are close to their families are happier than those who are not. People who participate in religious communities are happier than those who do not. Being connected to others seems to be much more important to subjective well-being than being rich."

There are physical benefits to having longstanding, intimate social connections, too. In a study with cancer patients, Dr. David Spiegel of the Stanford University School of Medicine investigated the effects of psychological and social variables on the survival of patients with metastatic breast cancer. His study showed that women who became involved in a support group where they could share their feelings not only experienced an improved quality of life and were more hopeful, but they actually lived longer. The women in a support group lived twice as long on average as the women who were not in a support group. (Both groups received state-of-the-art surgery, chemotherapy, radiation, and medications.)

As in so many other important life areas, it appears that women possess an intuitive sense of what this research tells us about the sources of true happiness. And again, the ways they organize their lives offer instructive models for society as a whole. While the prevailing ethos of our culture encourages ever-increasing affluence and freedom, the pursuit of these can easily result in a substantial decrease in the quality and quantity

# "Taking joy in living is a woman's best cosmetic."

## —Rosalind Russell

of our social relations. We make more money and spend it more quickly, but we spend less time connecting intimately with others. Schwartz reports that more than a quarter of Americans report being lonely — and that "loneliness seems to come not from being alone, but from lack of intimacy." Women, in their active pursuit of interpersonal connections and their involvement in social groups and institutions (churches, civic groups, charities, and the like) are taking important steps that will help them to avoid depression. Men, who are more likely to value autonomy and independence, have less of an innate defense against this crushing problem.

## the outlook on achieving what women want

Women's lives have never been more complex, multifaceted, and demanding than they are today. But from that complexity there is emerging a genuine sense of possibility. Their quest for balance, time, and control has given rise to a wide range of challenges for women, but also demonstrates that they have a wide range of life choices open to them. The decisions they are making, the truths they are finding on their journey, are having profound effects not only on other women, but on the men in their lives, too. Women today are teaching all of us ways to connect home and work, to use the lessons of one for the benefit of the other. They are discovering they can take care of others and themselves at the same time. They are proving that life isn't about making either/or choices; instead of one choice replacing another, one choice can enhance another. Their busy schedules are evidence that the spending of energy can sometimes produce more energy; that having multiple tasks can lead not to exhaustion but to increased vitality. Women's overwhelmingly optimistic outlook helps propel them to greater success and improved physical health. Their reliance on close, personal connections gives them a reliable source of trustworthy advice, a bulwark against depression, and an enduring foundation for building a happy and fulfilled life. As the women of today and tomorrow continue to discover and share their own values, the journey looks like it will be increasingly exciting and inspiring for all of us.

# • • • • • • Sources

Mary Catherine Bateson, *Composing a Life* (New York: The Atlantic Monthly Press, 1989).

Kathleen A. Brehony, *Living a Connected Life* (New York: Henry Holt, 2003).

Hilary Chura, "Failing to Connect: Marketing Messages for Women Fall Short," *Advertising Age,* 23 September 2003.

"Cooking Light Insight," *Cooking Light* magazine, 2003–2004.

William J. Doherty, Ph.D. and Barbara Z. Carlson, *Putting Family First* (New York: Henry Holt, 2002).

Mark Dolliver, "Days of Our Lives," *Adweek,* 17 November 2003, 90–94.

Anna Fels, *Necessary Dreams* (New York: Pantheon, 2004).

Bob Garfield, "Garfield's AdReview," *Advertising Age,* 12 May 2003.

Malcolm Gladwell, *The Tipping Point* (New York: Little, Brown & Co, 2000).

Hispanic Opinion Tracker, *People En Español* magazine, 2002.

Ann Hulbert, "Look Who's Parenting," *New York Times* Magazine, 4 July 2004, 11–12.

"Inside Style: The Mindset and Motivation Behind Women's Style Purchases," *InStyle* magazine, 2003.

Jeff Madrick, "Economic Scene," *The New York Times,* 10 June 2004, C2.

The Mom Connection, *Parenting* and *BabyTalk* magazines, 2004.

"A New Definition of Success: American Women Rewrite the Rules," *Real Simple* magazine, 2004.

Susan Nolen-Hoeksema, Ph.D., *Women Who Think Too Much* (New York: Henry Holt, 2003).

Kris Oser, "Moms Are Unsung Players in Gaming World," *Advertising Age,* May 2004.

Faith Popcorn, *EVEolution* (New York: Hyperion, 2001).

"The Power of Storytelling," *People* magazine, 2004.

*Real Simple* Problem Detector, *Real Simple* magazine, 2002–2003.

Barbara Bailey Reinhold, Ed.D., *Toxic Work* (New York: Dutton, 1996).

Barry Schwartz, *The Paradox of Choice* (New York: Ecco, 2004).

Michael J. Silverstein and Neil Fiske, *Trading Up* (New York: Portfolio, 2003).

*Teen People* Trendspotters™, *Teen People* magazine, 2003.

"Values and Behavior Outlook," *Real Simple* magazine, 2003.

"What Really Matters to Moms," *Parenting* magazine, 2004.

"Window on Our Women Report," *Essence* magazine, 2002.

"Women in Motion: Living Life on Their Own Terms," *Health* magazine, 2001.

## about the authors

**Grant J. Schneider**
is Vice President,
Brand Development
and Strategy, for the
Time Inc. Women's Group.

**Peter K. Borland**
is a writer and editor in New York City.